Pleasant Hill and Its Shakers

Pleasant Hill
and Its Shakers

Thomas D. Clark

F. Gerald Ham

Pleasant Hill Press

Pleasant Hill Press
Shakertown at Pleasant Hill, Kentucky, Inc.
3501 Lexington Road
Harrodsburg, Kentucky 40330

Library of Congress Catalog Number: 77-76515

Printed by Thoroughbred Printing, LLC, Lexington, KY
United States of America

Designer/consultant: Susan Jackson Keig, Chicago, IL

Photos: All historical photos, Historic Picture Archives, Pleasant Hill, with exception of p. 59, courtesy Elmer Ray Pearson, Chicago, IL, and p. 87, courtesy University of Louisville Photographic Archives, Louisville, KY. All other photos, James L. Ballard, Winnetka, IL., photographer, for Pleasant Hill.

Endsheets: Map of Pleasant Hill, (copy by George Kendall, 1835, of original made in 1834 by Isaac N. Youngs).

Page ii: Spiral stairway in the Trustees' Office.
Page v: Broomcorn held in a press to facilitate sewing into a flat broom.
Page vi: Doors to main entrance of East Family House; Brethren entered on right, Sisters on left.

Contents

Preface, vii
1 The Fermenting West, 1
2 The Founding, 8
3 Building Utopia, 15
4 The Day of Order, 22
5 On the Land, 27
6 The Shop, 35
7 The Serpent in the Garden, 43
8 Mother Ann's Work, 49
9 In the Course of Life, 55
10 Proselyting, 62
11 Wayfarers, 68
12 In the Tempest of War, 73
13 In the Seed of Time, 82
Epilogue, 93
Index, 98

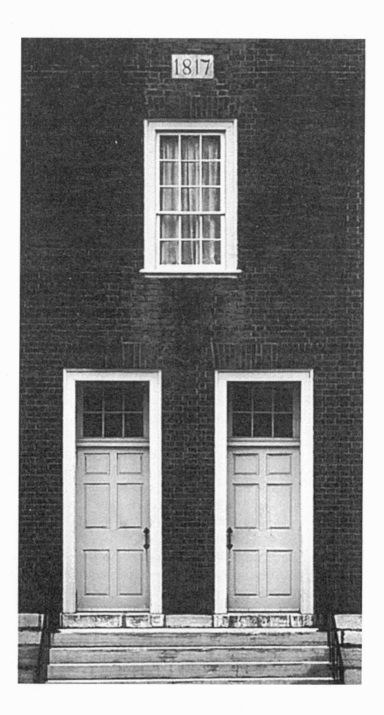

Preface

THE AUTHORS of this book know the story of the Shakers at
Pleasant Hill involves far more detail than is possible or
necessary in this book. More than any other Kentuckians of
the era covered by this history, the Shakers kept excellent
records. These deal not only with the day-to-day temporal
affairs of Pleasant Hill, but also with the spiritual activities of
the Society. Though not well-educated, the chroniclers were
observant and communicative in making their entries. As in
everthing else the Shakers did, the record keepers were
thorough.

This book is the brief record of one Shaker community,
one that differed in some respects from other communities of
The United Society of Believers in Christ's Second Appearing, more commonly known as Shakers. While the Shakers
subscribed to a form of withdrawal from the world, they were
tremendously fascinated by what went on about them. At no
time did their withdrawal have the isolative influence of
some of the Catholic orders. In many areas of their economy
the Shakers were very much in competition with their
worldly neighbors. Their farm produce, livestock, and handi-
crafts were prizewinners at the county fairs of Kentucky.
They found ready purchasers over a large part of the South
and expanding West. There still survives a respect for the
honesty of Shaker materials.

As a communal society, Pleasant Hill was doomed almost from the start. First, the rule of celibacy made it practically impossible to recruit enough converts sincerely dedicated to the teachings of Mother Ann Lee to assure continuity of the community. Second, the worldly forces were dead set against this type of social and economic organization. While there were local hostilities, it was the competitive forces of an aggressive American society which worked against the Shakers. Internally, demands for administrative management were often too great to be supplied by the Order. In the end, it was in this area that deterioration of the Society first showed itself. "Shakertown," or Pleasant Hill, stands not so much as a monument to a narrow religious concept of a celibate society, guided by a willful woman and a prevailing streak of spiritualism, as to the ever-recurring dream in American history that somewhere on this vast continent man could find a hallowed spot to achieve two objectives: first, the redemption of man from his original sin, and, second, the creation of the perfect society in which simplicity, integrity, and quiet love of one's fellowman could prevail free from the machination of a highly materialistic world.

This manuscript is based on the intensive research and writings of F. Gerald Ham. I, too, have examined the Shaker records rather extensively, but in the writing of this book I have depended on the excellent work of Dr. Ham.

THOMAS D. CLARK

1 The Fermenting West

KENTUCKIANS welcomed the opening of the nineteenth century with thankfulness that they had come through the ordeal of settling their broad land beyond the Appalachian Highlands. They had built cabins and substantial log houses, they had organized towns and counties, and on June 1, 1792, Kentucky became the fifteenth member of the Union. Menacing Indian attacks from both the South and North during the Revolutionary War had made pioneering an unusually bitter ordeal for many of the pioneers.

It was not until General Anthony Wayne and his army of carefully drilled backwoodsmen finally broke the back of Indian resistance north of the Ohio that the path to Kentucky was made really secure. Indian raids along the Ohio in the years prior to 1794 had taken many lives, but even worse they had created a state of fear which perhaps surpassed the actual danger from this source. The first three decades of Kentucky's existence were to leave a deep impress upon the state's history.

The turn into the nineteenth century brought certain satisfactions of accomplishment to the Kentuckians. By that time they had drafted two state constitutions; the second one went into force on June 1, 1800. At least two international conspiracies had been revealed and thwarted, and Kentuckians had spoken caustically against the Alien and Sedition laws, and the offending federal statutes had been repealed by Congress. Beyond these accomplishments the land of Kentucky was highly productive, and thousands of people who had come west with little more than packhorse loads of primitive tools and utensils were now prospering as farmers or merchants.

Pioneers who came through Cumberland Gap, or down the Ohio, brought with them a deep sense of religion. On two occasions whole church congregations came overland to found new churches, and to establish their particular faith in the new country. By 1800, the evangelical stirrings among the people were equal to the political excitement through which the new state was passing. Baptist and Methodist ministers were diligent in their labors. The Craig brothers, John Taylor, and many others, led Baptist flocks with zeal. Francis Asbury, the tireless Methodist circuit rider, later to become bishop, crossed and recrossed the Appalachians many times to preach to frontiersmen in Kentucky. There was a pronounced religious turn of mind in the state. Quieter Presbyterians organized congregations, and exerted a profound social and political influence in these formative years.

The years immediately following the opening of the new century were years of religious awakening. John Rankin, James McGready, and John and William McGee enthralled the people in western Kentucky with their highly emotional preachings along the Gaspar River in Logan County. Reminiscent of the earlier "Great Awakening" which had occurred east of the mountains in the middle of the preceding century, this new upsurge was to spread far afield.

During a warm August in 1801, in the pleasant, rolling meadowland of Bourbon County at Cane Ridge, Presbyterians, Baptists, and Methodists joined in one of the greatest religious revival meetings in the history of the Ohio Valley. People flocked to this meeting by the thousands. No one knows precisely how many, but possibly there were assembled ten to twenty thousand souls, perhaps the first time in frontier history that so many people had been brought together. Crowd psychology took over, and emotions arose to the breaking point. In fact, the throng lost control of its emotions as ministers preached around the clock. Using the vivid images of fallen and tormented men gleaned from Milton's writings, John Bunyan's *Pilgrim's Progress*, and from the *Old Testament*, the atmosphere at Cane Ridge grew sulphurous. There was shouting, screaming, dancing, praying, singing, jerking, moaning, and personal confessions. For some this was a moment of release of pent-up emotions, for others it was one of self-condemnation and great inward pain. The roar of the crowd was said to be like that of a mighty cataract.

Though men blended their voices and agonizing moans in a mighty crescendo of emotions at Cane Ridge, they remained willful and independent in their points of religious views. The Presbyterians were divided between those rugged conservatives who outdid Calvin himself in orthodoxy and those who wished to accept the spirit of revivalism. Among the latter were Richard McNemar, John Dunlavy, Barton W. Stone, Robert Marshall, and John Thompson. Philosophically, the separatists tended to place more faith in the teaching of Arminius than John Calvin. Thus it was that the Presbyterians found themselves divided in both view and spirit in a moment of religious revisionism.

At Cane Ridge men sought deliverance from sin by new formulas, and in their search they were ready to follow the teachings of any new voices raised among them. While Kentuckians debated their different approaches to saving man from his sins, three missionaries from the Shaker community of New Lebanon in upstate New York were on their way to the West in January 1805. Traveling through the Valley of Virginia they were drawn into the immigrant current down the eastern mountain shoulder and across the Appalachians by way of Cumberland Gap into Kentucky. Isaachar Bates and his two companions found the people in the new state of Kentucky ready to "suck in our new light as greedily as ever an ox drank water."

At the house of Malcolm Worley, an influential lay leader in the earlier Cane Ridge Revival, the Shaker missionaries found their target. Worley lived in the Miami Valley of Ohio and was a Presbyterian dissenter. Associated with him was Richard McNemar, a man of more than average intelligence and leadership ability. In Worley and McNemar the later apostles of Mother Ann Lee found two converts who could persuade others to embrace the faith. McNemar wrote, "For upwards of fifteen years my soul has been on the wheel, forming into union with professed followers of the lamb, but never did I find my mate, until I found the spirit from New Lebanon." By July 1805, John Dunlavy was converted to the Shaker faith and social philosophy, and with him came others who had belonged to one of the three major religious denominations in the Valley.

Behind the "spirit of New Lebanon" was a complex story of human frustration, a frantic search for liberation from the burden of corporal sin, and a reaching out for the perfection brought by complete salvation. Priestess of this "new light" theology of Arminianism was Mother Ann Lee. Mother Ann was born in the murky industrial town of Manchester, England in 1736. Her life story was little different from that of thousands of other impoverished English textile workers who earned just barely enough to keep body and soul together. The daughter of a blacksmith, Ann had no real advantages of education or any other forms of refinement. As soon as she was of school age she was forced to begin work in a textile factory. Growing up illiterate but diligent, she was sufficiently skilled to be trusted with the preparation of cotton and velvet fabrics, and later as a fur shearer in a hattery. No doubt many of the pelts which she sheared to make the plug hats of the eighteenth century had reached England from the North American fur trade.

As a teenage girl, Ann Lee left the fabric and hat factories for what was possibly more refined work. She was employed in an infirmary where she came to know a great deal about humanity. In fact, her jobs in the textile factory and the infirmary revealed to her the depravity and debauchery of human nature in eighteenth-century England. In search for an escape from the odious and sinful realities of life about her, Ann Lee yearned for certain assurances of the immortality of the soul. She sought these in simpler human terms than those put forward by traditional theologians. More important to her at the moment was the search for internal personal harmony in a life that was pillared on the social disasters of her age. She turned to a group of dissident Quakers for leadership. They were animated in their religious expressions and were convinced of the imminent return of Christ. Because of the vigorous physical expressions of their innermost feelings, these Quakers were called derisively "Shaking Quakers."

In these years when Ann Lee sought spiritual solace in a simple religious philosophy, she married Abraham Standerin, a blacksmith. She bore him four children, all of whom died in infancy. Following the death of the last child in 1766, Ann became more diligent than ever in her search for peace of the soul. Sexual coition to her was the lusty cross man had to bear for momentary pleasure. The unhappy experience at childbearing and in marriage to a heavy-handed, crude blacksmith, plus intense exposure to raw humanity in mill and infirmary and the emotional expression of the Quakers, caused the young woman to develop her own philosophy. Celibacy and open confession of sins were basic tenets. So militant did Ann Lee become in the promulgation of her newly-conceived doctrine that she disrupted worship in the local Anglican Church and was imprisoned in the house of correction in Manchester.

Imprisonment induced a more intense meditative state of mind. Thus, in a deeply thoughtful state in prison, Ann Lee formulated the basic theological belief that Christ would reappear in the female form. She began to receive spiritual visitations, and when she was released she was ready to assume mothership of the Shakers.

Mother Ann now looked across the Atlantic to the British colonies where she hoped space and primitiveness of environment would enable her to establish a new freedom for her views and followers. With a small band of converts, she sailed from Liverpool aboard the *Mariah* on May 10, 1774, for New York. This was a jubilant moment for Mother Ann and her disciples, even if the ship on which they sailed was a leaky old vessel unfit for such an extended voyage. At sea, a timber was ripped loose in the hull during a storm, but, miraculously, a wave slapped the plank back in place and saved the ship and its passengers.

The Shakers landed in New York in August just before the Continental Congress held its first meeting in Philadelphia. They found the colonies in an uproar over the rapidly approaching conflict with the mother country. Undaunted by the gloomy political outlook, the small band remained in New York City for several months before pushing upstate to settle on a cheap tract of swampy land at Niskeyuna near Albany. Here the celibate colony of Believers set the pattern which was to characterize Shaker organization in all the other American communities of Believers.

The first responsibility of the immigrants was that of erecting family cabins and opening farmlands from the heavily wooded swamp. By fall of 1776, the sect was settled down on a farm and had the land in production. Nevertheless prospects for making converts in the New York backcountry were dim. It was not until a series of revival meetings occurred that it was possible to establish the New Lebanon community on the New York-Massachusetts border. In this colony the Shakers were able to proselyte a band of millennialist Baptist dissenters who had been greatly aroused in a recent revival. They were willing to accept Mother Ann as the reincarnation of Christ, and later to subscribe to her communal plan of celibate living.

Yet all was not smooth sailing for the Shakers. Throughout their history they were to face the problem of war and military involvement. Almost immediately after their arrival in America they were caught up in the emotionalism caused by the outbreak of the American Revolution. Because of their pacifist attitude toward war, members of the Niskeyuna community were thrown into jail and Mother Ann was threatened with banishment to England on a charge of treason. Instead of hurting the Shaker cause this baseless charge of subversiveness to the cause of independence aroused widespread sympathy, and helped to draw in fresh converts from Massachusetts and Connecticut. Within a decade nine New England societies, or communities, were founded.

Poverty, imprisonment, deprivation, and over-exertion took their toll of Mother Ann. Ten years after landing in America she died at forty-eight years of age in Watervliet, New York, on September 8, 1784. Her death caused some defections, but leadership of the Believers was assumed by James Whittaker, Joseph Meacham, and Lucy Wright. Once again the Society of Believers gathered momentum. This time, perhaps, the gospel of Mother Ann became more impelling than ever because it came from the hand of the dead and could not now be materially revised.

In 1787, the new leaders of the Society instructed the faithful to assemble, preparatory to gathering into Orders, and to forsake the world. This eventually meant the collectivization of property, the dissolution of marriage vows, and a full confession of sins. On Christmas Day of that year, the faithful gathered in a communal assembly to confess their sins. They began the processes of surrendering their claims on worldly goods, accepting celibacy, and formally separating themselves from the world. They were now prepared to greatly enlarge the work of Mother Ann by going abroad through the land to search for converts and to form new communities. Their mission was that of preaching a gospel of peace for the human spirit and contentment for the mind in an atmosphere of love and mutual assistance. They were not to be bound by the fundamentalism of some of the more orthodox denominations, or to be burdened by seeking after material things in an aggressive competitive society.

2   The Founding

THE SOCIETY of Shakers, or Believers, had succeeded in up-state New York and New England by 1792. Eleven communities gave every indication of thriving, and prospects were bright for expansion. Now the Society began to look far afield to the ever-broadening American frontier as a land of rich harvest. On January 1, 1805, three colonizing missionaries set out generally for the western country, by way of the Valley of Virginia, to seek new converts.

Between the beginnings of settlement at Harrod's Town and the middle of the first decade of the nineteenth century the western trails and rivers poured a constant stream of settlers across the mountains. People of all economic stations, and all sorts of turns of minds made the journey to find fortunes in the rapidly expanding West. Despite the emotionalism stirred by the booming revival of 1801 there were plenty of immigrants who were still without religious commitment.

The organized churches which had come to exist in Kentucky demonstrated a sharp denominational partisanship. The Scriptures were narrowly interpreted and many religious efforts became so involved in the charged lines of theology that frontiersmen were at a loss to understand their point. There was a sexual lustiness no doubt in the region, but sexual intercourse, when it was promiscuous, met with scorn. This scorn did not go so far with the traditional religious groups as to suggest celibacy, and sex as an unforgivable sin. The one thing the newly-opened West needed was manpower, and a large family was as much a sign of thriftiness as a well-tended field or a well-stocked smokehouse. Much of the legal structure of the newly-formed state centered about marriage, children, and the descent of property. This was an intimate part of Kentuckians perpetuating themselves in the land.

It was in this kind of social and religious climate that the first Shaker missionaries were rebuffed. To begin with, the religion of Kentuckians was male centered, and male administered. The idea of a female counterpart of Christ was anathema. Fortunately for the visiting Shaker, Benjamin Youngs, and the recently converted "New Light" leaders, Richard McNemar, Malcolm Worley, and John Dunlavy, they found three men from Mercer County who were willing to listen to the testimony of the new gospel. They drew aside from Barton W. Stone's Cane Ridge Church to a private house where Benjamin Youngs presented the doctrine of Mother Ann Lee.

This meeting in August 1805 marked the beginning of the Pleasant Hill community of the Shakers. In the next year, converts began to gather themselves into a communal family on Elisha Thomas's 140-acre farm, located on the historic Shawnee Run just off the waters of the Kentucky River. Early in December 1806, the faithful gathered there and accepted the first family covenant. They agreed to mutual support, and to a common ownership of property after each individual's possessions had been listed. Forty-four converts of legal age signed the original covenant.

High above the deeply slashed gorge of the palisades along the Kentucky River, the faithful located their seat. Here in the beautiful meadowlands of Mercer County, the new religious order sat astride the scene of the historic beginnings of Kentucky. Not far away, in 1774, James Harrod and his party of long rifle hunters had come on their journey to the head of the Salt River to locate Kentucky's first permanent settlement. By 1806, all around the new Shaker village were the homes of some of Kentucky's earliest and most prominent settlers. Within this territory Indians and pioneers had stalked each other across the rolling terrain in their bitterly fought contests for possession of the land.

In a remarkably short time the 140-acre nucleus of Elisha Thomas's homestead grew into a baronial-sized domain of 4,369 acres. Much of this land was of top quality and it was almost impossible for an industrious people to fail economically in its use. High above the Kentucky the level limestone plateau placed the Shaker location in a pleasant air current which favored man and crops. The loam soil had grown progressively more fertile, being fed from beneath by centuries of decaying limestone, and from above by a rich vegetable cover which added humus.

At the Shawnee Run location there was abundant fresh water, virgin timber, stone, and clay aplenty. It is difficult to convey an impression of the magnificent stand of timber in this area. Black walnut, cherry, ash, oak, tulip poplar, and towering sycamores, all added to the wealth of the region. It was a situation which loosed the imagination of the builder and cabinetmaker. The Kentucky River was an open channel of transportation for bringing coal from upstream, and shipping products of the farm and shop southward.

Between the old frontier settlement of Harrodsburg and the rising western city of Lexington, Pleasant Hill was on the main axis of a rapidly expanding economic community. Paradoxically, the socially and economically withdrawn Shaker community was in the path of resistant forces. These arose largely out of jealousy over the well-being of the Pleasant Hill community which could not have been more visibly evident in any other part of Kentucky. That Pleasant Hill was founded and thrived in its Mercer County location is a monument to Shaker thriftiness and ingenuity.

In the fall of 1808 the outline of the present village was staked off and a log house was built on the site of the later location of the Centre Family Ministry. The Kentuckians wished to assume full administrative responsibility of their own spiritual and economic destinies, apart from Union Village, Ohio. A ministry, or ruling body, was established that comprised the Easterners, John Meacham, Mother Lucy Smith, Eldress Anna Cole, and Elder Samuel Turner who served as the elders and eldresses of the first family. A second family was located in March 1809 a mile to the east, under the administration of Willis and Joanna Ballance. This new family lived in a lean-to shed of the most primitive frontier kind. The land for this family's use had to be cleared of heavy timber, and a more permanent house built. At the same time scattered members had to begin the long and arduous process of gathering into communal order.

By April 1812, three communal families, East, Centre and West had been organized. A fourth, the North Family, was established as a "gathering family" through which new converts were passed on their way to becoming permanent communicants. Now the communal organization was in a happy stage of progress. The hierarchy was established with a central ministry: the families were directly under the supervision of the two elders and two eldresses, and various labor responsibilities were under the direction of supervisors or work deacons and deaconesses. Each family constituted a semi-autonomous economic and living unit with its dwelling house, barns, shops, herds, and fields. Each had control over its products, but always with the knowledge that the families shared their goods. In case of a local calamity or crop failure, the community still had central economic planning.

By now the membership and complexities of the community had expanded, and there were four families. No longer did the Shawnee Run Family Convenant cover the needs of the growing community. It became necessary to draft a new communal agreement which would take into consideration the times of expansion and the broader demands made on the Order, and which would make some sense of the political state in which the Order existed. On March 10 of that year a new joint community compact was formed which provided for the general welfare and common good of the Society. A clearer statement of the tenets of the

Order was made, and principles of internal and external, or worldly, relationships were stated. By giving four months notice, members could secede from the covenant and take their listed goods with them. They could not, however, make a claim for wages or increments earned during their stay. It was considered that the seceder had consumed these in living in the community. Wisely, the Society voted to admit no new members who were encumbered with debts.

It was evident from the beginning of the community that the Shakers would not live on and cultivate such fertile land industriously without creating urgent needs for commercial relationships with the outside world. They also had need for funds with which to make capital improvements. Both their fields and their shops produced goods which had to find a market. James Gass and Abram Wilhite were appointed elders to transact the Society's external business. These men became salesmen for Shaker products and purchasing agents for goods which the Order had to buy.

The communal society in America had a difficult time living within a political state and a skeptical community without incurring certain animosities. At the very moment that the Pleasant Hill community began to succeed, Kentucky became deeply involved in the War of 1812. Local emotions ran high and attitudes toward the peace-loving Shakers were critical if not hostile. The Shakers were never ardent pacifists, but they did not take part in wars or military exercises. In these politically troubled years the younger leaders at Pleasant Hill had begun to take their places in the Order, and the Believers generally were becoming more steadily fixed in their faith. Had there been no war this would still have been a moment of trial with the Shakers' Kentucky neighbors. The latter were critical and suspicious of the Shakers' communal celibacy. It was hard for them to conceive of a group of people living in such close association without being guilty of sexual promiscuity. A bill was introduced, and failed of passage by the Kentucky General Assembly in 1811, which attempted to interfere with Shakers educating their children within the strict rules of their Society. The following year a second law

Shaker children, Brethren and Sisters are pictured in stereographic view of the second North Lot Family House, built in 1831 on the main road, with stables and sawmill opposite.

was enacted which provided that an unbelieving spouse could secure a divorce, custody of the children, and a portion of the property involved.

As previously mentioned, the Shakers were pacifists, a privilege which neither neighbor nor state respected. They were called upon to pay fines or bonuses with which to hire substitutes for the militia. Refusal to pay the levies resulted in seizure and sale of Shaker property by the sheriff of Mercer County. Later in 1815, however, the Kentucky Court of Appeals ordered the restitution of the property and upheld the Order's freedom of choice about military matters.

Despite the tribulations of critical neighbors, the war frenzy, and adverse legislation, the Shakers thrived both economically and spirtually in the early decades of the new century. The community settled down to the order of things to the extent that a much stronger compact could be formed.

On June 2, 1814, a compact which required a final, irrevocable surrender of private property, and a full personal dedication to a solemn covenant with God and with fellow members was signed by 128 Believers. This convenant launched the Pleasant Hill community as a full-fledged communal society, after the pattern established by the Mother Colony of New Lebanon, in the commitment of the Believers to the faith and teachings of Mother Ann Lee. Three trustees, James Bryant, Francis Voris, and Abram Wilhite were made legal stewards or trustees to manage the extensive property of the Society.

The Shaker Order in Kentucky had reached by 1814 a state of some maturity. Now the challenges of the Shakers reached well beyond the matters which had concerned them in the formative years. The land was to be brought into maximum production, trade with the outside world was to be established and expanded, and most important of all, so far as the local community was concerned, permanent buildings, in conformity with the plan or religious and social organization of the Society, had to be constructed.

3   Building Utopia

ONE OF THE most ingenious young men to live in the West in 1815 was Micajah Burnett. This youth came close to being a genius in the fields of engineering, architecture, and administration. He had been brought into the Society of Shakers in 1809 by his parents, when he was seventeen years of age. Six years later, the twenty-three year old convert proved himself mature enough to begin the realization of the Pleasant Hill dream of providing adequate permanent structures to house the families and their activities. He laid out the village with its great family houses, a meeting house, craft shops, utility sheds, and barns.

Burnett's plan for housing the families called for three large structures facing on a village street. The first of these was approximately 55 by 45 feet, and was three stories high with a towering attic on top. Across the rear was a dining and kitchen ell measuring 30 x 60 feet. The house was based on a heavy limestone foundation which enclosed a deep basement. The walls were constructed of native bricks, and the trim, of stone quarried on Shaker property.

To carry out Burnett's ambitious plans it was necessary for Shaker workmen to busy themselves in rock quarry, clay pit, and woods, assembling the materials for such massive structures. They cut stone from the cliffside of the Kentucky River Gorge, burned limestone to make the lime, formed thousands of clay bricks, hewed and sawed the heavy beams which went into the superstructure of the building, and sawed and dressed the flooring and finish lumber. The quality of the timber can still be viewed in the fine ash floors of the East Family House.

Within the remarkably short time of three years, 1817-1819, the East Family residence was completed. By 1822, the West Family House was constructed. Young Burnett had gained experience in the erection of massive buildings. He worked largely with native and maybe initially unskilled labor, and with raw native materials. He had no access to specialty milling plants, stone dressing shops, or to supply houses for custom-made materials. Soon after the West Family House was finished, work was begun on the construction of the large Centre Family unit. A three-story structure built on a 55 x 60 foot foundation to which is appended a 34 x 85 foot dining room and kitchen, this building was to replace the third Centre Family dwelling built in 1812-1815.

The lines of the Centre Family building differ somewhat from those of the neighboring family houses. It has square gabled ends and three massive chimneys. It was not until 1834 that this building was completed and ready to accommodate over 100 occupants. Delay in construction was caused partly by lack of funds but primarily by dissension within the community itself.

Burnett did not busy himself with the construction of three large residences alone. Between 1810 and 1834, barns, shops, a laundry, a tannery, a water pumping and supply station, and other outbuildings were constructed. In this period Burnett and Tyler Baldwin built the excellent gristmill and the stone fulling mill. Perhaps there were no other barns or general farm buildings in Kentucky before 1840 which were so large in size or so well-designed and constructed. The builders not only sought to create shelter for their animals, products, tools, and crafts, but to give them a high degree of efficiency and permanence. Foundations were laid with stone as were those in the great family houses. It took an enormous amount of manual labor to hew the heavy framing

Centre Family House, begun in 1824 and not completed until 1834, was built of limestone quarried in nearby Shaker quarry.

beams and to saw the large amount of lumber needed for walls and flooring to say nothing of the labor needed to construct the buildings themselves.

In many respects, the most ingeniously designed and constructed building at Pleasant Hill is the clapboard Meeting House. Externally this is the least impressive of the main buildings. External appearances, however, are deceiving. Micajah Burnett was confronted with the challenge of erecting a building which would contain a room large enough to accommodate the membership of the Society. Because of the ritualistic nature of Shaker worship the great hall had to be free of central obstructions. Supporting stanchions in the large room would be both obstructive and hazardous in the processes of the dance form of worshipping. Because of the vigorous physical expression of emotions which took place, the walls and superstructure of the building had to be strong enough to withstand an intense amount of vibration.

The Meeting House was constructed in 1820. It is 60 x 44 feet and rests upon a heavy limestone foundation. The walls are suspended on an intricate framework of heavy studding and plates of hewn timbers. The roof and ceiling are supported or suspended on a series of interlocking cantilever-type trusses and overhead studdings and rafters. The ceiling cross beams are suspended from above by tie trusses which distribute a good part of the weight on the rafters.

An exploratory visit to the attic of the Meeting House reveals a superb job of notching, fitting, and balancing of cross members. Actually much of the weight stress is relieved in the carefully notched joints. In a century and a half the Shaker Meeting House has stood the vicissitudes of weather, insects, instability of Central Kentucky soils, and the hard usages of Shakers and the subsequent tenants who have worshipped here. There is now no appreciable evidence of a weakening of timbers, or of other types of deterioration. The woodwork in this building is comparable if not superior to that in any of the standing ancient English manor houses.

In design, the buildings at Pleasant Hill give certain external evidences that Burnett was heavily influenced by the then popular Federal style of public architecture as well as by a central design of Shaker buildings approved by the New Lebanon ministry. This design permitted him to provide a maximum amount of space with a minimum amount of cutting and arranging of internal walls and stanchion supports. It was possible to design with relative ease for the administration of a celibate society which was co-sexual in organization. Separate entryways could be provided without marring the general appearance of the facades of the buildings. Internally, separate dormitory quarters could be established in keeping with the external forms of the building.

The family buildings at Pleasant Hill contain cavernous amounts of space in their deep cellars, and in the broad attics under the spacious roofs. Space of this type was of the utmost importance to serve both the living arrangements of the Order and its domestic economy. These buildings were the scenes of almost beehive-like activity.

The interior arrangement of stairways, halls, and rooms reveal both thoughtful planning and excellent craftsmanship. There was constant awareness of functional uses of the buildings. Beyond these facts there is an astonishing amount of lightness and cheerfulness in what was designed to be a plain if not austere setting. By combining an early nineteenth-century angular fashion with a certain religious severity, the Shakers achieved a sedate grace, if not always of form, then of internal order.

Micajah Burnett gave way to an almost intoxicated spasm of romance in designing the stairways of one of the buildings. The twin spiral staircases in the Trustees' Office are marvelous examples of suspension, as much so as that in the attic of the Meeting House. Both the superstructure of the stairwells and the curved railings reflect a mature knowledge of geometrical angles and curvatures. More difficult to achieve was the bending of the cherry rails to conform with

View of east side of the Meeting House, with entrance to the second floor living quarters of the two Eldresses in the Ministry.

graceful pre-set symmetry of three flights of winding stairs without use of sophisticated tools and bending processes. The stairs are tied into the building at the foot and landing stages, and at the top.

Whether or not Burnett was responsible for the internal decor of the Shaker buildings is not clearly known. Perhaps the scheme which came to prevail was adopted partly out of the tenets of the Order, and partly because of the exigencies of housekeeping in which so many people were involved. A special tone of blue paint, prescribed from New Lebanon, was used throughout as trim on certain of the buildings. Walls were painted an off-white or were whitewashed. Floors were plain with perhaps some kind of waxing material spread on them. Walls of the rooms were lined with pin-boards from which extended turned pegs of uniform length and design. These were used for hanging candle sconces, clothing, utensils, and even pieces of furniture. The rooms

Fanlight over doors leading from the refectory, shown with Shaker stove, to kitchen area in the Centre Family House.

further revealed the desire to keep good housekeeping order by the location of closets or wardrobes, often built in.

Outside trim of the buildings revealed the same meticulous care to details as the interior design. Rainwater was caught in gutters and drained down into stone "rain catchers" which delivered the water well away from the buildings. Stone steps, window copings, iron guard rails, all were solidly constructed as were the walkways.

Thus the physical community of the Shakers became a model of rural farm planning and building. Whatever their Kentucky neighbors thought about the strangeness of Shaker religious practices and social philosophy, they were thoroughly convinced that the Believers were industrious, ingenious, and orderly. At no time in Kentucky history has any group of people demonstrated a greater capability of using raw, local materials to achieve such notable results. This fact alone served as an invaluable demonstration of what native people could achieve by applying their wits and energy.

All of this tireless activity was carried on at a time when the Shakers were most devout in their physically vigorous ceremonies of worship. The dances, although a form of spiritual release, were taxing of human energy, and it is hard to imagine a worker taking vigorous part in the religious exercises and then being in condition to perform efficiently the next day in the handling of heavy building materials. It was also a period in which much administrative and counseling energy was expended on bringing converts into submission with the commonwealth, and in proselyting for members.

4   The Day of Order

IN SOME DETAILS the Shaker community at Pleasant Hill did not always conform to the more intricately ordered and stricter organizational regimen of the older communities in the East. There was a greater casualness about the community. No doubt part of this stemmed from the temperamental and sectional differences of the people in the new West. It was not as difficult to secure listeners to the preaching of the gospel of Mother Ann as it was to institute the internal rules of the Society passed down from New Lebanon, and Union Village, Ohio, the ruling ministry in the West.

The growing Society at Pleasant Hill between 1810 and 1830 also had a desperate need for manpower to bring its lands and shops to full production. The only way to grow in numbers was by proselyting for new members in Central Kentucky. John Dunlavy had been an early "New Light" revivalist and he knew the turn of mind and emotional natures of his neighbors. He came from Union Village, Ohio, to travel in Central Kentucky where he preached the Believers' doctrine.

Dunlavy, the missionary, met with moderate success in swelling the ranks at Pleasant Hill. His services to the Order, however, extended beyond his missionary work. He was scribe and theologian, producing *The Manifesto*, a publication representing the views of a largely self-taught biblical scholar who was able to harmonize the teachings of Shakerism with the Scriptures. At the same time it was a sharp stricture against the writings and teachings of such stalwart frontier theologians as Barton W. Stone, Lorenzo Dow, and others.

At Pleasant Hill, John Dunlavy proved to be a man of marked versatility. He was village physician, father confessor, preacher, and novitiate master. At one time he had under his watchcare 140 young Shakers who were being led along the path to becoming confirmed Believers.

The Pleasant Hill communicants were slow to conform with the more regimented Church orders of some of the other communities. Not until 1817, did they, for instance, separate the covenant members from the new converts. They all lived together, and this, said the New Lebanon ministry, worked against the strength of faith of both groups. The basic plan of the Shaker community depended upon the division of the people into classes based on their spiritual progress, somewhat in imitation of the Jewish temple. There were three classes of Shakers: the novitiates, the junior class, and the senior or Church order.

The novitiates were a noncommunal group made up of the new converts who had accepted the faith but who had not fully undergone the emotional experience of breaking marriage and family ties. The junior class was little different from the novitiates except they were usually unattached children who had no family or emotional ties outside the community. Sometimes they brought property with them and were in the process of surrendering it as they advanced in religious instruction. Finally, the senior classification included those who had made a final dedication of their time, talents and property. The last order was composed of those who had signed the Covenant of 1814.

In 1817, the Pleasant Hill Society met internal criticism by separation of the community in the order of worship. The Shakers were Sunday worshippers, the more advanced Believers meeting at nine in the morning. In these services they not only listened to sermons but they also gave free range to physical expressions of dancing, singing, and clapping of hands. The younger classes were called together at noon on the Sabbath and were given religious instruction without the same rigorous physical exercises.

In the village the family organization underwent extensive change. Elderly members of the East Family were moved to the West Family residence. The contention on the part of Father Joseph Meacham of New Lebanon was that this removed the older members who had lived "longer after the flesh" farther away from the physical attractions of youth. Too, in the division of labors, the older Believers were given tasks which were less taxing physically.

By a separation along lines of age of the West Family, there was created a second senior order within the Society. This new order shared fully in all the activities of the religious Society and in the economic benefits of the prospering community. In 1834, the Centre and East Families were formed into the first order of the Church, a confirmation of the fact that the religious Order had undergone material advancement in maturity and dedication.

Unlike Catholic orders, the Shakers at Pleasant Hill were never fully able to maintain the strict order of their classes. They were never able to establish the novitiates into an ideal integral part of the community. In fact the Shakers never promoted this idea with energy. They purchased two or three outlying farms and established conjugal families on these farms. A communal structure was constructed on the Denny place near the Elisha Thomas farm to accommodate several converted families during the decade 1820 to 1828. Some young converts were housed on the Louis Varner farm, and a third novitiate station was located on the Bricky Farm in 1824. By 1830, the scattered novitiate residences were abandoned, largely because members had left the Shaker faith.

In the place of the experiments with the intermediate states of the novitiate residence and the family house, there was instituted the "Gathering Order" which had its own house overlooking the Kentucky River Gorge on the northeast side of the village. The Shakers instituted the Gathering

The West Family Sisters' Shop, located at the rear of the West Family House, shows Georgian style influence in its design.

Order to initiate nonfamily converts to the communal organization of the Society. Here young Believers were gathered under the watchcare of John Dunlavy, Betsey McCarver, and Virginia Congleton. The house, opened in November 1817, was known as the North Lot Family House.

A second gathering place of an increasing number of novitiates was a group of log cabins east of the North Lot Family House. Later, in 1821, these new converts were moved into a house on the Kincade tract of land to form the West Lot Family. Again the newly-converted Shakers were separated from the seasoned Believers for physical and administrative reasons. Each Gathering Order maintained some independence from the other, being administered by its own stewards and trustees.

This was a period of schism—building construction had more to do with the general level of prosperity and maturity than with any prospering of the Gathering Order which suffered heavy membership losses at this time. The first residence constructed for this order was the West Lot Family House which was a lesser copy of the West Family structure, except it was built of stone. It was smaller, housing only fifty persons. Its internal arrangements were similar to the West Family House to the detail of the kitchen and dining ell. In 1831, the larger brick North Lot Family House was built on the same lines of the West Lot Family House to complete the physical organization of Pleasant Hill village. Sometimes the elders must have had doubts as to whether or not their efforts with restless young novitiates were well-spent. Frequent were the desertions of these youths, many of whom had come to the Order as homeless orphans.

There was a paradox in the combination of Shaker religious philosophy and economic endeavors. To the cynic standing by and listening to their preaching, and observing their antics at worship, they appeared to be ephemeral, nonsensical people who had lost touch with reality. No matter how emotional or absurd many of their apostate Kentucky neighbors were, the Shakers appeared downright foolish. If contemporary Kentuckians could have read some of the entries in the journals detailing worship experiences, they would have branded them lunatics.

On the other hand, it is doubtful if any Kentuckians were better planners, and more skilled and tireless workers than were the Shakers. Most of all, their labor activities revealed a kind of hard sense and practicality then largely unknown to the West. Their construction of a village of large buildings within two decades was in itself a monumental accomplishment. Along with this they were among the most successful farmers and craftsmen in the Ohio Valley. But the Shakers knew well there was a very intimate connection between the vitality of their economic life and their spiritual well-being.

5   On the Land

AS CONVERTS came into the new Shaker community, some may have brought with them deeds to farmlands, and numerous heads of livestock. The great plantation surrounding the Pleasant Hill village was acquired mostly by purchase. In their acquisition of lands, the Shakers, who were first Kentucky frontiersmen, demonstrated a hardheaded practicality born of long experience before they became Shakers. The land was of sufficient size to permit large-scale farming and a high degree of diversification. No other communal society in America was located on more fertile soil, or in a more propitious situation to be self-sustaining.

The land at Pleasant Hill produced crops of wheat, rye, corn, flax, tobacco and hemp. The vegetable gardens produced bountifully, and by 1811 the Society had planted orchards which in time would bear an abundance of fruit for both home consumption and the outside market. Heavy demands were made for vegetables throughout the year. Members of the Society became highly proficient in preserving fruits and vegetables, and in storing vegetables for winter use.

Farming in Kentucky in the first half of the nineteenth century tied the state's economy to the developing Lower South. The Kentucky River by way of the Ohio and Mississippi formed an artery of transportation all the way to New

Orleans. By the end of 1816, a new gristmill was constructed on Shawnee Run and in January 1817 began grinding the Society's corn for market. All up and down the river and along the side branches there were mills grinding meal and flour, but perhaps none of them was so ingeniously equipped as the Shaker mill. An elevator was constructed in such a way as to carry grain to the top of the mill where it passed through three sets of grinding stones on its way down. Three times the grist made the journey through the burrs before it was ready for packing.

A mechanical shucker and sheller was devised which enabled the miller to shell four hundred bushels of corn a day. In order to carry on year-round milling operations, another mill site was purchased at the mouth of Indian Creek. The new mill was inaccessible by wagon. To solve the problem a chute was built to feed the grain into the top of the mill by gravity.

The mills solved the processing of grain. The Shakers then had to construct boats to transport their products downstream. The first crafts were the conventional flatboats which plied the western waters before the steamboat came into general use after 1820. The first boat under the command of Francis Voris, Abram Fite, and Robert Barnett departed the Shaker Ferry at Shaker Landing for the Falls of the Ohio in February 1818. This Ferry, the first of two owned by the Shakers, was located about five miles northeast of the village.

Other farm products were prepared for market at the mill. Flax was a major crop and clever millwrights devised a horse-drawn braking machine. It consisted of a set of fluted rollers and a large wheel equipped with knives along its rim which broke or "singled" the flax as it rolled over it. This machine was far more productive than the clumsy hand brakes or hackles used by the Shakers' neighbors. As much as 4,000 pounds of flax in the stalk could be run through the mill in a day. The fiber was used in the weaving of linen cloth, and as the warp for making the heavy linsey-woolsey fabric which was so popular in Kentucky and the South. The most important byproduct of processing flax was linseed oil.

Hemp was handled in the same way. This latter fiber was used for making coarse cloth, sacking, and wrapping and bagging for cotton bales. The lands of Pleasant Hill were ideally suited for hemp production.

All sorts of products were prepared for the market from the farm. Symbolic of the Society's energy and ingenuity were the Shaker brooms. These, like the grist of the mill and the fiber of the braking wheel, were sold over a wide territory. Shaker peddlers, like their famous Yankee counterparts, were seen everywhere with their bundles of brooms. They, no doubt, introduced the "patent" or manufactured broom to literally thousands of housewives along the Ohio and Mississippi shores. This homely household item continued to be a consistent piece of merchandise throughout the years the Society sold its products.

Sometime in the early half of the century, the Shakers began the sale of garden seeds. Until the outbreak of the Civil War, seed peddlers plodded through the western country in late winter and early spring selling their wares. Although there is no evidence that the Shaker gardeners knew anything about plant genetics, they did know the importance of plant selectivity, and for this reason, among others, they developed a reputation for honesty in merchandising, and for the results which their seeds produced. There may have been another fact which gave them a good reputation. Their gardeners were willing to engage in the growing of a wide variety of vegetables. There is clear evidence that the Shakers lived well, and that their larders were well-stocked most of the time.

Despite the fact that the Society of Believers was ostensibly withdrawn from the world, they were not unaware of trends in various areas of American agricultural and domestic economy. In South Carolina and some of the other southern states, farmers began experimenting with growing silkworms. The fact that the mulberry tree thrived across the South made it seem that the region promised to be as good a silk-producing country as the Orient. Silkworms were imported into the country and for a time the industry showed promise. The Shakers brought silkworms to Pleasant Hill, possibly as early as 1816, and for a time they produced cocoons for their own use, and produced an excess of sewing silk which they peddled to customers along with brooms and garden seeds.

Not only the cultivated fields produced abundantly, but so did the pleasant meadow pasture lands. Livestock grazing is one of the oldest economic activities in Kentucky. In fact the McAfee brothers in 1774, and James Harrod's party, quickly discovered that Central Kentucky was ideally adapted for development of a livestock industry. When settlers began moving over the trails to the West, they brought with them their droves of hogs, flocks of sheep and herds of cattle.

Unhappily, the early livestock brought into pioneer Kentucky was of poor quality. Inbreeding in the years following did nothing to produce animals equal to the quality of pas-

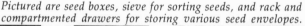

Pictured are seed boxes, sieve for sorting seeds, and rack and compartmented drawers for storing various seed envelopes.

turage available. When converts came into the Society and brought their farm animals with them, they did little to promote a successful livestock program. It became necessary for the Shakers to begin an active breeding program in order to establish a profitable grazing activity. In 1811, and in conjuction with the Union Village Society in Ohio, they purchased a purebred English Shorthorn bull. This bull, named "Shaker," was one of the earliest, if not in fact, the first purebred bull to be brought to Kentucky. Six years later the Society profited from the Lewis Sanders importation of English breeding stock.

By the 1830s, livestock production had become a major source of income. It had come to supplant the growing and milling of cereals as the main source of income. After 1830, the Shaker herds were steadily improved both by importation and selective breeding. In 1832, the Society's herd was diversified to include imported English Durham cattle. The Shakers joined Henry Clay in the importation of the bull "Orizimbo" which cost one thousand dollars. Later they cooperated with Union Village in importing purebred bulls from Scotland. Not only did the Pleasant Hill community cooperate with Union Village in the importation of animals, but also there were constant exchanges of animals with other Shaker villages, a fact which went far toward improving herds.

Elder John R. Bryant was an alert herdsman. In the 1850s he attended cattle sales about Kentucky, and especially those held on R. Atchison Alexander's famous Woodburn farm. In 1856, Brother "Rufus" Bryant was a judge in the first Kentucky State Agricultural Fair.

Not all the Believers' cattle were of the beef type. They built up a good herd of milking Shorthorns. These cows were said to have averaged eight gallons of milk a day. Butter and cheese (4,000 pounds a year) were shipped down river in large quantities. It was with sound reason that Elder Joel Shields wrote in 1834, "Our cattle are considered by stockraisers to be very good," and "Our full-blooded Durhams are in great demand, but we cannot spare any of them yet."

There came a time when the Shakers did sell surplus animals. In 1832, they derived eighteen hundred dollars from cattle sales, and in 1857, six thousand. If the published lists appearing in herd books are true indications, the Shakers of Pleasant Hill had the largest registered Shorthorn herd in America in 1850.

When American hog breeders near the Mother Colony of New Lebanon imported the Berkshire breed of hogs in 1832, the Shakers immediately adopted this type of hog for their use. Two years later, the Berkshire was sent out to the Miami Valley, and then to Pleasant Hill. The Pleasant Hill boar, "Black Hawk the Great" was said to be the finest one in Kentucky. The Believers did not confine their interest to Berkshires alone. They imported several other English, Scotch and Irish breeds. They benefited from Union Village's development of the Poland China breed from crosses with the "Wood" hog to produce the "Warren County" breed. Within a decade and a half, the Pleasant Hill drove of purebred hogs numbered 500 head, and the Shakers enjoyed a good income, approximately twenty-four hundred dollars a year, from the sale of pork. An interdiction against the Believers eating pork, issued in 1848, destroyed the hog-growing project of the colony.

Attempts at producing on the land, in the shops and in the households all of the raw and finished materials possible, forced the Shakers to raise sheep. Their pastures were ideally suited for the purpose. By 1829, they were importing purebred animals from England and Scotland. They brought over the Leicester, or Bakewell, breed to cross with other Kentucky stock. This resulted, said Trustee Bryant, in the production of a superior meat carcass and a fine quantity and quality of wool. The new Shaker breed of sheep adjusted well to the Kentucky climate, and thrived on native grasses.

By 1850, the Pleasant Hill Shakers owned 1,060 head of sheep from which they fleeced 3,400 pounds of wool annually. Following the spring shearing season, the families pooled, weighed and divided their wool. This marked the beginning of the arduous process of washing, burring, carding and spinning the wool into yarn.

A tremendous amount of draft power was needed to work the large plantation, to harvest hay and crops, and to serve the grain mill and other farm needs. Aside from these needs, building materials had to be hauled, sometimes over considerable distances and over steep roads which necessitated increasing the number of horses and oxen. The Believers gave serious attention to the breeding and training of draft animals of good quality. In a region where people regarded horses with reverence, the Shakers were no less proud of their teams. They, however, did not produce the lighter weight, sporting-type thoroughbred. In another way they did not follow the popular trend in Kentucky of producing mules. They regarded the hybridization of animals a preversion of the natural order of creation.

In light of the Believers' attitudes toward human sexual intercourse, it is an interesting fact that they paid so much attention to the breeding of high-quality farm animals. In the field of animal husbandry they enjoyed an unusually fine reputation for excellence. This was an apparent contradiction of their beliefs, whether or not the Shakers accepted the fact.

By no means was the Society of Believers shut off from the mechanical and technological changes which were taking place in America in the first half of the nineteenth century. They quickly adopted new tools and farming implements as they became available. They made improvements in many of the tools and machines. From their own shops came ingenious devices for lightening the burden of farming. In the harvest season in July 1847, a company of fifty-seven men and boys went into the grain field with the Purviance, "West Wind," drawn by four horses, to garner the new crop. This machine was the latest thresher type propelled by a series of wooden cogs. Within an eleven-hour day it cut and threshed 630 bushels of wheat. In addition to this new machine, the Shaker Orders owned six reaping machines, a cylindrical rake, a mechanical mower and a corn planter. Thus, Pleasant Hill proved to be a testing ground for new machines as they came on the market.

In the late 1850s the Shakers attempted to fill one of their domestic needs for sugar by introducing Chinese sugar cane to Kentucky. In 1858, they operated two iron roller cane grinding mills and produced 564 gallons of syrup of the sorghum type, used largely in the making of preserves. Syrup making, however, did not prove to be one of the Shakers' most successful farming activities. Actually the Shakers had to purchase sugar from the outside to meet their heavy demands.

For more than half a century, 1810-1870, the Society of Believers proved itself a thrifty, progressive, agricultural body. Under excellent management the farms were highly productive. Barns and cribs were filled in successive crop years with bountiful harvest. Shaker farm animals were exhibited at Central Kentucky fairs with fine success. For the area the Society was an excellent farm demonstration community as well as a religious Society. No one can assess the influence the Shakers exercised in causing their Kentucky neighbors to adopt better cultivating and breeding procedures on their farms. Up to the great panic of 1857, the Shaker farmers were prosperous. After that period, however, their economic fortunes changed. The era of the Civil War added further crises to farm operation, and by 1865 most of the momentum gained in earlier years was lost. Farm operations dwindled, profits took sharp drops, and farm management became less efficient and imaginative as the internal affairs of the Society itself became more involved in changes and frustration.

The lands of the Pleasant Hill farms were less productive in the declining years. They were neglected because the Society found itself short of the management skills and labor supply necessary to continue a progressive and high-level farming operation.

6   The Shop

SHAKER CRAFTSMEN were no less successful in their shops than the farmers were on the land. There is ample evidence remaining in the buildings and their furnishings that some members of the Society became highly proficient in woodworking. As noted earlier, carpenters and joiners did excellent work in the construction and trimming of the buildings. The wall trim, cabinets and closets all present evidence of clever handiwork.

Furnishings for the rooms, though of simple lines and design, required a good amount of skill to produce. Fortunately, there was available, either from trees on the farm or from along the Kentucky River, a wide variety of excellent woods for furniture making. This necessitated a selection of trees to be cut, sawing of the lumber, and considerable care in its seasoning.

Saws, lathes, drills and glueing racks were installed in the woodshops. Parts of chairs and cabinets were planed and shaped by hand. Posts, spindles, and rounds for chairs, tables and beds were turned largely on foot-propelled lathes. Holes were drilled by use of hand-operated brace and bits.

One of the best known and handsomest pieces of furniture made by Shaker craftsmen was the chair. These were built basically on two or three designs—some of them at Pleasant Hill resembling in a remote fashion the popular

Windsor type. Chairs in large numbers were made to supply the buildings. The commercial chair was solely produced by the Eastern Shakers.

Beds of various types were manufactured in the shops. These were single beds, some double beds, and the low trundle beds which could be pushed out of the way during the day. Designs were plain, of good taste and highly utilitarian. Chests and cabinets were of sturdy, plain construction, built to give long and hard service without reflecting the grace of line and ornamentation of the more fashionable commercial types of the period. Tables, for instance, were sturdy, constructed of beautiful woods, but demonstrating the craftsmen's devotion to order and utility rather than to line and style.

The cooper's shop workers devoted much of their time to the making of all sorts of wooden household wares. From the years the first pioneers began housekeeping at nearby Har-

Clothes presses line the walls of the attic in Centre Family House, lighted above by double dormers across the roof ridge.

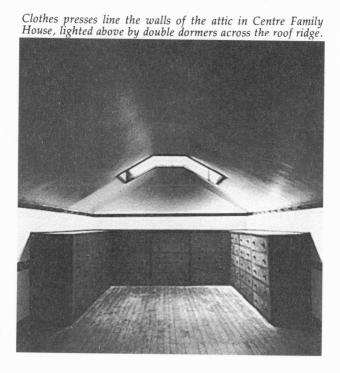

rod's Fort until the post-Civil War period, Kentuckians made constant use of two small wooden vessels known as piggins and noggins. The Shakers manufactured these out of cedar wood, and offered them for sale along with their other wares: a whole line of tubs, churns, buckets, and keelers.

Appearing on sales invoices were "most fancy baskets" which no doubt were woven out of thin white oak splints and willow reeds, and like the cedar buckets, had a multiplicity of domestic uses. Not only did experienced weavers create baskets, but they likewise wove the seats of chairs with oak splints. Willow branches were gathered along the Kentucky River from which the baskets were woven. It is possible that the fanciest baskets were made from these branches from which the bark had been stripped.

Oftentime journeys into the woods to gather oak splints and willow branches were also for the purpose of gathering tanbark. The Society used considerable quantities of leather in the making of shoes for members, harnesses and saddles, saddlebags, whip lashes, and curtains for covered wagons. The Shakers may have sold leather goods in their public trade, although little or no mention is made of this fact in the Society's journals. To condition hides, there was a tanyard of some size.

Along with the production of leathers, the Shakers produced their own cordage. Hemp was one of Kentucky's main crops before 1870, and much of the fiber from this plant was twisted into ropes. The needs of the village for rope and cordage were considerable. Beds were suspended on a cross winding of cord. Outside, rope had scores of uses in farm operations. Hempen fibers were twisted in a ropewalk, the mechanics of this twisting device were simple indeed. A strand of hemp was fastened to one side of a revolving cross bar, and the spinner walked backward attaching bands of fiber as he went. Single strands were then attached to three or four wings of the winder, and as many twisters as there were strands walked backwards while the winder drew the strands into tightly woven ropes.

Items listed for sale on invoices included sugar boxes.

Whether this meant the boxes were to be used in the coagulation and drying of maple sugar, or as storage boxes is not clear. Also listed for sale were carpenter's gauges, and miter and angle-cutting guides.

Shaker craftsmen were as clever as Yankee clockmakers in the use of woods. Heavy demands were made by the family houses for all sorts of gadgets ranging from simple wall pegs to shuttles, looms, sleys, and furniture. They experimented with the making of common household items such as clothespins, flat brooms, boxes, and dry measures.

The flat broom with its turned handle became a symbol of the Shakers' mechanical ingenuity and practical design, and also of their commercial sense. Wherever the name Shaker was known people had a high regard for their brooms and brushes. Although the art of broom making is an old one, the Believers produced an unusually strong sewn broom which supplanted the old bunched rush or straw brooms of the South and West.

Shaker inventions went beyond the manufacture of household and farm items. The Believers built machines which greatly facilitated the production of standardized materials and objects. They used the circular saw at an early period, and built a splint-shaving machine. These were either inventions or innovations of the Eastern Shakers.

The Shakers were not unwilling to labor long hours in the performance of heavy labor, nor were they opposed to using labor-saving devices. In 1831-1833, they installed a gravity force water supply system. This consisted of a wooden tank mounted on three stone piers. The water was lifted by a horse-drawn pump. Leaden pipes were laid to the community kitchens, cellars and wash houses. The wash houses were equipped with horse-powered washing machines which relieved the laundresses of the laborious necessity of scrubbing and battling clothes. Perhaps this was the first such water system installed in Kentucky.

Female members of the Society were as clever in their work as were male craftsmen. They busied themselves by making a long list of things for the use of the Society and for

The "World's People", who often came to Pleasant Hill to buy flat brooms, pose with the industrious Shaker Brethren and workers at entrance to Broom Shop.

sale. They were adept at making palmetto bonnets, straw hats, mattresses, pincushions and willow baskets. They must have worked diligently in the creation of these things because their invoices indicate rather large quantities of handmade items in Shaker cargoes.

A necessary function of the Shaker Sisters was the production of cloth and garments from the wool and vegetable fibers produced on the farm, and from the raw cotton which was bought in the South. The list of types of cloth was a fairly extensive one. There were linen, worsted, linsey-woolsey, drugget, flannel, and a lighter domestic used to make garments, blankets, quilts, sheets, curtains, towels, bonnets, hats, strainers, sacking, and wagon and carriage covers.

Shaker garb was rather formless and drab, made of brown, gray and blue standard shades of cloth. Men dressed in baggy linsey-woolsey trousers, linen shirts, heavy split-tailed coats, broadbrimmed hats, coarse home-woven hose and squaretoed shoes. The Sisters did not present themselves as fashion plates even in nineteenth-century rural Kentucky. Their dresses were of various muted colors with long, loose-hanging skirts and long-sleeved, collarless waists, and an additional kerchief, or bib. The Shaker bonnet was at once a hat and a broad sunshade which gave the Sisters the appearance of being almost ageless in their uniformity of dress. Stockings and shoes differed little if any from those worn by the men.

The most that could be said for Shaker clothing was that it was warm and durable. It apparently had little or no sale on the public market. This was not true of the textiles, however. Before 1840, there was a ready market down river for all the cloth the Society could produce. Linsey-woolsey was in popular demand for the making of slave and coarse work clothes. Other types of more supple and refined cloth were sold for the making of dresses and other garments. In 1840-1842, the Sisters of the Society produced approximately a thousand yards of carpeting annually.

Dr. John Shain had the watchcare of the growing of the Society's medicinal herbs. The garden, however, could not produce all the supplies to meet the demand of the trade. There were certain wild plants which supplemented the cultivated garden sources. At certain seasons, the Sisters went to the neighboring woods to gather herbs. Among their harvest were horehound, lobelia, sarsaparilla, liverwort, snakeroot, bloodroot, mayapple and other plant roots and seeds. Some seasons in the early 1840s the Sisters gathered, dried and processed 2,500 to 3,000 pounds of medicinal materials to be sold in the southern trade.

Good food, like solidly built furniture or sturdy brooms, was a matter of pride with the Believers. Except for the later interdiction against the eating of pork, and use of tea and coffee, there were no other food taboos or austerities. They were excellent cooks, lavish with their ingredients. Vegetables from sixteen gardens were available in limitless quantities. Grain supplied meal, flour, and other forms of cereal. Meat from the fine collection of cattle, sheep and poultry was never in short supply, nor were eggs, milk, cream, and butter. Shaker cooks took genuine pride in their art, and their communal meals were of high quality. One visitor said of the "Kitchen Class" at Pleasant Hill, "In the art of cookery, they excell any people with whom I have been acquainted." A Cincinnati newspaper reported, "more glorious cookery—I have never met with."

Fruits, berries, and vegetables were converted into jellies and preserves, and the delights of the Shaker kitchens were sent far afield. These were packed in glass jars holding approximately three and one-half pounds and placed in boxes holding a dozen jars. In 1855, the three Church families realized $10,250 from sale of preserves alone.

Honesty and skill in the manufacture of their products brought the Shakers an enduring reputation. Long after their coopersware, baskets and preserves were off the market, people remembered their fine qualities. Quality alone however could not keep the Society in a competitive position with

te 19th century photo of Shaker Sisters and visitors at the then derelict Fulling Mill, built 1822 on Shawnee Run Creek, with wooden aqueduct to carry water to the mill.

the outside world. It was difficult if not impossible for the Society to develop and retain within its membership enough craftsmen to carry on a constantly-advancing manufacturing business. As the general American manufacturing process was impoved and mechanized, the Shakers found themselves incapable of competing. A rising use of textile machines, for instance, made hand carding, spinning, and weaving of wool too slow and inefficient a process to permit competitive pricing. As new types of cloth came from the New England mills, textures and types of textiles changed, bringing about changes in the types of garments worn by the old jeans and linsey-woolsey customers.

Introduction of more sophisticated woodworking machines such as planers, shapers, mortises, and drills increased the supply of furniture while lowering prices. The widespread use of the steamboat tended to remove the old barriers of effective distribution of manufactured goods which narrowed the margin of profit to a level below which the Shakers could make a profit.

After making such a promising start toward succeeding with a highly diversified domestic organization, the Society was unable to hold its own. The crushing weight of American progress was against the Order. Nevertheless, the Shakers were able to make some economic adjustments and adaptations to changing times. It was internal dissensions, slackening of administrative controls, and a general state of decay that brought ultimate economic failure.

7   The Serpent in the Garden

THE SOCIETY of Believers was an equalitarian body in the sense that no distinction was made between individual members. Elders labored as diligently as did neophytes. Theological beliefs were intimately associated with manual labor, and work was a joint virtue. This concept of necessity demanded an internal organization and division of labor in the community. It was imperative that the extensive lands be made productive, and because most of the converts had farm backgrounds, it was not difficult to develop an agrarian economy.

Though work was looked upon as a spiritual and virtuous act, it was more important as a fact in sustaining the Society than as a central doctrine of the Order. To the Shakers, labor was a creative force indicative of personal consecration. Mother Ann Lee did not work out the complete details of labor procedures; this was done by succeeding elders. A community planned an economy in harmony with the region, and was allowed a certain amount of leeway in its operations. Part of this came from the fact that conditions of farming varied considerably between the East and West, but also because of the individual community approaches to management of its internal affairs. There was criticism by some of the visiting elders that the Shakers at Pleasant Hill deviated, in several small phases of life in the community, from central ideas of the Society.

The entire Shaker community differed in many respects from the nature of other types of utopian communities on the American frontier. It lacked the stern patriarchal domination of George Rapp's socio-religious community in Indiana on the Wabash, at New Harmony. Nor did its leaders seek to emphasize an intellectual purpose as did Robert Owen in later years, also at New Harmony. By the very nature of the Shaker community, there was no real concern with any type of social reform. In their own missionary activities the Shakers were ardent laborers. The Society was not adverse to taking in new members or to the establishment of new communities. No attempt was made by the Society to live completely isolated from the worldly community.

The biting panic of 1819 seriously affected the tenor of life at Pleasant Hill by disrupting the sale of products and manufactured goods. From time to time, acts of the Kentucky General Assembly, whether aimed directly at the Order or not, had a bearing on life in the community. No doubt the restlessness of the people of Kentucky during the years when there was a constant movement to the new lands of the expanding West had an unsettling influence on the younger Shakers. Too, the influences of equalitarian Jacksonian democracy had impact on the Shaker membership.

On September 16, 1826, Elder John Dunlavy died from severe malarial infection. He was on an extended visit to the West Union community in Indiana at the time. It was a serious loss to the leadership at Pleasant Hill. During the intervening years (in 1818) both the temporal and spiritual guidance of Pleasant Hill fell into the hands of Mother Lucy Smith who enjoyed a distinct dominance over Second Elder Samuel Turner. Within five years, the serpent of dissension had shown its head.

A willful young convert, John Whitbey entered the faith in 1818, and by 1825 had become interested in the social doctrine of Robert Owen. His discussion of these beliefs to the discredit of those held by the Shakers resulted in dissension and the ultimate expulsion of Whitbey. He had a last say

The Trustees' Office, after restoration, where commercial and legal transactions were permitted with the outside world.

with the elders before his expulsion in November 1825, by accusing them of being not only arbitrary in their treatment of him, but, even more fundamentally, of being oppressive and despotic. He wished to see the elders and deacons elected by popular vote. This reform was instituted, but it did not allay internal dissatisfactions.

In January 1827, the ministry, elders, and deacons voted to effect a new administration at Pleasant Hill. Lands, goods, and property were placed under the oversight of family stewards. No longer were the village trustees accountable to the ministry, but rather to individual families. This new arrangement, however, did not bring peace to Pleasant Hill. James Gass and Tyler Baldwin went to New Lebanon in 1827 to seek confirmation of the new order. Their mission was a failure. The Kentucky community was now believed to be in disharmony with the central doctrines and orders of the communal pattern established by New Lebanon. The New

Lebanon ministry instituted quick and positive action to allay a revolutionary impact on the Pleasant Hill community.

Delegations of the ministry and elders were sent from Union Village and New Lebanon to quiet the dissension at Pleasant Hill. These visitors or delegates arrived at various dates in the summer of 1827. In their opinion, the Order was in a highly-disorganized state. Infidelity and apostasy were rampant. Young Shakers were disillusioned. Wordly influences flowed into the Order almost without hindrance, and the system of stewards was not working.

A program of reform was begun instantly. Management of internal affairs was returned to the village trustees who managed transactions with the outside community. An equal division of proceeds from products and goods was made to the families. Mother Lucy, grown weak both in mind and body, was relieved of her responsibilities. James Gass asked for a property settlement and left the Society. This removed from the community a pioneer member but also a highly controversial one in later years. The real loss, however, was that of young people. By 1830, only a handful of youth was left.

The delegation from New Lebanon restored religious order. Members resumed the confessions of sins, and waywardness was halted. By late 1828, the community was progressing and practicing once again in "union" with the central beliefs. This restoration was not accomplished without the serious loss of forty-two pioneer members of the faith who departed the Society. One reason given by some of the apostates was that they had failed to find the perfectibility of men and spiritual surcease which Mother Ann's gospel had promised.

These departures raised a more serious question perhaps than mere loss of leadership. Some of them sought to reclaim their property. Citing Kentucky law they declared the property of Pleasant Hill was held in joint tenancy to which departing tenants were entitled to a share. They made this claim despite the fact that the Shaker community was unincorporated, and the General Assembly had first to enact a law establishing control over the community. The dissenters' cause was strengthened in April 1828 when Samuel Banta, a highly-respected member of the Society, seceded. A suit was brought before Circuit Judge Bridges of the Lincoln County Circuit under the title *Gass and Banta vs. Wilhite et. al. A Society of Shakers* in 1831. The Judge dismissed the case which involved the technicalities of the lack of corporation of the Society, and the possibility of recovery of property. The Shakers also were sustained by the Kentucky Court of Appeals.

The Kentucky General Assembly enacted a law February 11, 1828, to regulate civil proceedings against organized communal societies, thereby subjecting the Pleasant Hill Shakers to civil proceedings in the courts. All the sheriff had to do in issuing a summons was to affix a copy of the document to the Meeting House door. The leaders at Pleasant Hill immediately contended this was a constitutional violation of freedom of conscience. Richard McNemar, dispatched to Pleasant Hill from Union Village to assist in the legal troubles, wrote five booklets in which he reviewed the rights of the Society to conduct its affairs according to the tenets of their religious doctrines. It was clear to the Shakers that if the law was upheld by the courts, their community could not survive. Seceders would bankrupt it by their lawsuits to recover property claims.

The elders wisely turned to Senator Robert Wickliffe of nearby Fayette County to represent them in an unsuccessful attempt to get the 1828 law repealed. In the meantime, the Meeting House door was defiled by the tacking up of court orders. On April 6, 1829, the case *Banta and Gass vs. Wilhite* was tried in the Lincoln County Circuit Court. After an enormous number of records were accumulated in the form of depositions, the case was dismissed in 1831 because the plaintiffs were unable to support their contentions with admissable facts.

Success in the lower court did not end the litigation. The next year the contention of the seceders was carried to the Kentucky Court of Appeals. In an interesting exchange of arguments by contending attorneys concerning the nature of the Shaker convenant and the Commonwealth's position in regard to internal religious squabbles, the Appellate Court ruled the apostates had no right to make a claim.

The court decision sustained the central fact of Shaker communal organization. The litigation had cost one thousand dollars, but the Pleasant Hill elders desperately needed a favorable ruling to check the continuous efforts of seceding members to collect their property, and even of claiming compensation for their labors. In addition to the legal fee, the Society paid thirteen thousand dollars to the recalcitrants.

To further strengthen the Order's position in the future, a new convenant was drafted by Richard McNemar and was signed by the membership on May 20, 1830. The document, however, was supplanted almost immediately by one drafted for general use by the New Lebanon ministry in the East. This general document was signed at Pleasant Hill June 10, 1830. It was not until 1844, however, that Pleasant Hill covenant was brought into full conformity with the central rules of other Shaker Societies.

Thus, after a period of bitter contention the Pleasant Hill community was again united in purpose. From 1835-1860, the Society returned to a condition of "ordered living." These were, in many respects, the golden years when the community prospered spiritually and economically.

New leaders were selected, and they gave stable guidance to the Society for several decades. Among these were James Rankin, who succeeded Samuel Turner as head of the Order. Assisting him were Amos Ballance, Sarah Jenkins, Paulina Bryant, Micajah Burnett, Elhanon W. Scott, and Benjamin Bryant. Most of these new officers were second generation Shakers.

8 Mother Ann's Work

DURING THE period 1820 to 1860 large numbers of Americans were caught up in one form of spiritualism or another. They sought a means of communicating with departed souls, with God, Christ and the Prophets. They also sought glimpses into the future. The *Old Testament* contains accounts of divine visitations, visions, communications, and prophecies. It is not at all strange that the Shakers were captivated by spiritual communication and "union." Mother Ann Lee's death was but a transitional phase in her role as the female incarnation of Christ. The Believers thought she would return to instruct them in the "minutes of faith and practice by open vision, by direct divine revelation."

In 1837, a class of young girls at the Watervliet, New York community were strickened by strange shakings and whirlings. They claimed their spirits departed their bodies and were wafted to the celestial Kingdom to be given a guided tour by Mother Ann herself. This separation of corporal body and spirit spread among the various communities. The spiritually elected, visionists as the Shakers called them, were able to produce songs, poems, and exercises, all of unexplained normal origin.

At Pleasant Hill in September 1838, Sarah Poole was the first to experience the sensation of being a disembodied spirit. She manifested the change in her state of being by whirling around like a top until she dropped to the floor. In this state she was accompanied to Heaven by the occupants of the Shaker cemetery where she was shown the celestial sights, and given songs and poems.

Following Sarah Poole's experience, there occurred a rash of physical separations, visions, and visitations. The journals during the years of spiritual excitement contain entries which surpass belief. All sorts of messages came from Mother Ann, Christ, and other faithful, departed Believers. These messages often were in the form of admonitions against extravagance, carelessness in work performance, idle talk, lust. Mother Ann perhaps appeared more forceful and authoritative in her spiritual visitations than if she had actually visited Pleasant Hill in person.

The being of the spirit was expressed in other ways. Two peculiar and imaginary forms were the bushes and balls which appeared as gifts to individual members. Bushes were presented by angels and were loaded with gifts of oils of limberness or other physical attributes. The spiritual balls offered an even greater variety of blessings, and, when popped by an elder, would distribute Mother Ann's love, gospel freedom, simplicity, fire, indignation, good order, and fidelity. All sorts of gifts were distributed by the heavenly elders through their earthly representatives. Sometimes visiting elders from other Shaker communities would come bearing spiritual chests which were filled with treasures of virtue, and which were handed out to everyone. A list of these gifts was almost endless. No pirate chest ever contained such a variety of blessings. There were celestial rakes, crowns of wisdom, gold watches of thanksgiving, lamps of righteousness for the young, bottles of oil of salvation, boxes of gospel seeds, and even rods of fire.

This era was one when Shakers became more withdrawn from the world. They adopted taboos against eating pork and the use of coffee, tea, and tobacco. In this connection it may have been true that the Shakers, like many of their Kentucky neighbors, at one time distilled liquors and brandies from their grains and fruits. The inspired *Millennial Laws* received in New Lebanon in 1841 soon were extended to Pleasant Hill. In almost every case these served to tighten rules relating to diet, relations of the sexes, and closer supervision over children. These new laws in fact attempted to institute rules of simplicity, sobriety, austerity, and purity.

As time passed, the lines of Shaker discipline and worldly separation became more clearly defined. Reflective of their millennial tendencies were the instructions for the communities to select spots to be sanctified. At Pleasant Hill the Believers restricted the point of contact with the outside world to an entryway through the Trustees' Office gate, and this was guarded by an angel with a flaming sword. Further, the Pleasant Hill Shakers chose their secluded holy place where the soul could bathe and be refreshed in seclusion.

On September 21, 1844, the Holy Sinai's Plain was located by divine inspiration. This spot was a half-mile southeast of the Meeting House, and not far from the present route

The Shakers held their religious dances and services, Sundays, in the large unobstructed first floor of the Meeting House.

of the public highway. In 1844, this place was well-away from
easy public gaze. The spot was graded and sodded in blue-
grass. It was enclosed behind a fence and adorned with two
fir trees. On Thanksgiving Day 1844, a holy trek was made to
this place, and once a year after that. This trek was a full-dress
parade of the community accompanied by heavenly parents,
an angelic host, and departed members of the village. At Holy
Sinai's Plain the various classes would step forward to be
cleansed at the fountain and to receive gifts of virtue. One of
these was in the form of psalms written on invisible
signboards and read by the inspired. On Christmas Day
1844, God himself appeared at Holy Sinai's Plain. For the
Shakers it was truly a day of soul-searching and awesome
judgment.

Coupled with all the other spiritual manifestations were
numerous visitations from prominent historical figures,
North American Indians, and peoples from out-of-time or
around the globe. Personal visitors seemed to have been
limited only by the Shakers' imagination and knowledge of
history. A sampling of historical visitors included George
Washington, Benjamin Franklin, William Penn, and General
LaFayette. These persons came to Pleasant Hill and participated actively in worship ceremonies. Occasionally one of
them, like George Washington, took an active hand with the
elders in lecturing the Society on decorum and fidelity.

No visitors, no matter how prominent in the heavenly
hierarchy or in world history, created more excitement than
the endless procession of Indians. Both chiefs and braves
came to visit. Some of them misbehaved badly, even to disrupting the separation of the sexes of the Order. In this
obsession with Indians the Shakers reflected some of the
contentions of Joseph Smith and the Mormon concern with
aborigines. Some of the Indians who came to Pleasant Hill
proclaimed themselves members of the Lost Tribes of Israel.

Lost "Children" of Israel or not, the coming of such
well-known chiefs as Powhatan, Cornstalk, Bluejacket,
Tecumseh and others, were extraordinary events. Intermixed
with the children of the American forests were Turks, Arabs,

Africans, Irishmen, Eskimos, Chinese, and Latin American Indians. All of these acted out their nationalistic or racial character. They all had one thing in common, they sought salvation and looked to the Shakers to point them the way. It was a joy to the Believers when they saw the visitors respond, and it was not so joyful when they failed to do so.

Like all visitors, the exotic and heathen visitors brought gifts. Indians brought buffalo skins filled with love, and chestnut and chinquapin bushes covered with many delights. In turn, the Shakers gave honey, corn meal, and parched corn. Records of aboriginal visitations reflected a naivete on the part of the Shakers which bordered on the formulas of the dime-novel description of Indian character.

Perhaps a psychologist could explain the fact that the mediums were able to act out the parts of the various ethereal visitors. No one could predict the moment when the visitors would appear. This was especially true of the Indians. Sometimes an uncouth brave would appear in the midst of a service and disrupt the proceedings with his antics. The mediums would act out the moods and behavior of these rude visitors even to the extent of doing war dances, shouting, jumping, and shrieking. At other times Indian visitors were shy and withdrawn. All of them, no matter what their behavior, received religious inspiration and light in the faith. A constant query of the wandering spirits was, "What can I do to be saved?"

The involvement of the Shakers at Pleasant Hill was interesting because it reflected their awareness of what was happening elsewhere in America. There could be no doubt but what their indulgence in such vigorous spiritual activities was a form of vicarious escape into the world. In the obstreperous Indian visitor who ran roughshod over the meeting, the medium no doubt was giving way to a similar desire to rebel. There were other incidents in which the Believers seemed to reflect a desire to escape the restrictions of an ordered society.

This revealed a close affinity between the predictions of William Miller that the second appearance of Christ would occur in either 1843 or 1844. The prediction coincided in large part with those pertaining to the reappearance of Mother Ann Lee. Actually a movement was underway for a union of forces in observing the approaching millennium. The Shakers recruited approximately 200 members from Millerite ranks. One of these was Enoch Jacobs, editor of the adventist *Day Star*. The association, however, was of rather short duration, and Enoch Jacobs and the *Day Star* wandered elsewhere to find spiritual solace.

There were other spiritualists who attracted the attention of the Shakers. Among these were the toe-cracking and fraudulent Fox sisters who claimed ability to communicate with the world of the spirits. In 1853, a Dr. Graham from Washington arrived at Pleasant Hill with his "rapping" daughter Mary to set off a rage of table rapping. The Believers entertained Elizabeth Young, the healing and writing medium from Boston. These quacks not only entranced Mother Ann's children, but also many other Americans. At least the Shakers did not seem to have been taken in by the traveling phrenologists of the era.

By the late 1840s the Shakers began to taper off in the field of great spiritual excitement and to concentrate more on gaining converts and the perfection of worship ceremonies. Nevertheless, the spiritual period in which "Mother Ann's Work" was an active fact was one of the exciting periods of Shaker history. Entries for this period in the community journal are about as good documentation for the emotional and spiritual issues which stirred America as can be found. Still it is difficult to relate the emotions of the Shakers to the rather prosaic conditions then prevailing in Kentucky.

9 In the Course of Life

FOR A MODERN visitor walking through the buildings at Pleasant Hill and up and down its village street, the first question he wants answered is that of the course of life in the village. There is visible on every hand evidence that the Shakers were industrious people. Like the Puritans of New England, they regarded work as a virtue and a spiritual necessity. Every phase of activity in the colony was planned with a high degree of precision. At four o'clock in the morning during summer months and at five in winter the village bell was rung to awaken the Believers. The Brethren left their rooms within fifteen minutes to perform feeding and other outdoor chores. The Sisters straightened up the rooms for all the residents.

For about an hour and a half both sexes worked at their morning tasks and then returned to their rooms for a brief rest of ten minutes before marching down to breakfast two-by-two, the males in one line, and the females in another. After a silent grace they sat on long benches at separate tables and ate their meals in silence. Then the Believers were ready to begin their labors in shop, laundry, and on the farm. Their tasks were as numerous as were the activities of the village.

The morning period of labor was approximately six hours in summer, and five in winter. The marching formation was repeated for the noon dinner. By one o'clock laborers were back at their tasks to work until the bell called them in to supper at six o'clock. Evening family worship, when held, was preceded by half an hour of meditation.

Society today has found the Shakers' practice of celibacy a puzzling philosophy. There is plenty of evidence that extraordinary efforts had to be made to prevent carnal lapses within the families. Men and women were thrown into close daily associations, and they lived under common roofs. Methods were devised by which the two sexes had "union together" without having sexual relationships.

These "union meetings" consisted of organized conversations in which two rows of males and females, matched as to age and spiritual experience, sat facing each other in a line three feet apart and carried on hour-long conversations on prescribed topics or joined in singing. Private unions were forbidden as were strong male-female attachments. On evenings when there were no union meetings, families provided other modes of relaxation and union, consisting of instructions in new ways of laboring, in dance, in new songs, in testimonies, or in spiritual teachings.

The Shakers were strict Sabbatarians. Families assembled evenings in union meetings (eight o'clock in the summer, nine in the winter) on Tuesdays and Fridays; on Mondays, Wednesdays, and Thursdays they met and practiced songs and other parts of the religious services. At ten on Sunday mornings they gathered in a church meeting.

The main religious service occurred at one o'clock. When the big bell was rung, Church families and the Gathering families marched in pairs to the Meeting House with the elders and singers in the lead. The men marched ahead of the women, each sex entering the church by separate doors. Inside, members were seated on long benches with the sexes facing each other.

The presiding elder directed the worship service. When he signaled the beginning, the worshippers formed themselves in columns on opposite sides of the room. An opening anthem of marked solemnity was sung, and then the tempo was increased. Before 1850, preaching, when it was done, was by John or Benjamin Dunlavy and often for the benefit of the visiting public. Few souls were saved in the worldly evangelical sense and emotions remained calm in the dispensation of these messages of love.

The real excitement of the Shaker worship service was manifested in the dance. It might begin with a step and shuffle, and then a swirling circular set. A Virginia visitor to Pleasant Hill in 1825 said, "The air was filled with piercing shrieks, shouts, and confused acclamations of Bedlam." In-

An inspirational inscription below the music without words, in this personal song book of Elder Benjamin Dunlavy, reads: "The Apostle Paul to Benjamin Dunlavy, May 20th, 1845."

side the church he found about 130 worshippers, black and white, drawn up in ranks of eight abreast and seven or eight deep. The Sisters were assembled along the west end and the Brethren along the east wall. The men pulled off their coats and two singers from each column began the song and dance. Then, said the visitor, "the singers commenced and the columns got into motion. They gently advanced and receded for some minutes, when on a sudden, they reversed fronts, quickening their motions and danced in a similar manner; suddenly they wheeled to their former positions, increasing in the violence of their actions, as they were warmed by the spirit and animated by the singing. By one impulse they now broke the order in which they stood, and each column whirled within its own limits, in vertical commotion, throwing their heads, hands, and legs in wild disorder, occasionally leaping and uttering a horrid yell." The dancers joined the singers, "and all were singing with stunning violence; presently the two small windows near the ceiling, were seen partially and gently to open, and the face of a male and female were imperfectly presented at the opposite windows. (The Virginia observor here refers to the small apertures located halfway up the enclosed stairway at either end of the room. From these points the ministry could observe the progress of the dance. Thus it was impossible for any irregularities to occur on the floor undetected.) At this instance the motions which were before violent, became furious, until their violence, and the incessant fury of their dancing exhausted the worshippers. Some sank on the floor, whilst others were scarcely able to get to their seats. The worship closed, and I left the house with feelings of horror which you can better imagine than I can describe. The singing was *Vox Nil Praeterea*, 'sound without word, rhyme or sense'."

This was a vigorous way to spend the Sabbath. Later at five-thirty another family singing exercise was underway in which members learned new songs. Many of the songs were composed locally and were sung in somewhat the old primitive Baptist style of lining-out songs. During the 1840s, the village's chief composer was Samuel Hooser, an ex-Methodist minister. The songs were amateurish, often praising Mother Ann, or expressing momentary emotions of the composers.

It is not difficult to imagine the curiosity and gossip the Shaker services stirred up in the surrounding Kentucky countryside. Stories of all sorts were afloat as to the frenetic form of worship of the Believers. On occasions the worship services were opened to the public. Printed notices were sent ahead announcing the fact. The Shakers believed that by opening their doors they could proselyte new members. Visitors had first to listen to a sermon by the public minister outlining Shaker beliefs. Sometimes as many as one thousand visitors came for the public services. They often crowded the Meeting House so tightly the dancers were severely limited in their full expressions of their dances. These public meetings were pitiful gestures because they failed to do little more than provoke derision. Very few if any converts were made to the Society. In November 1869 the public meetings were discontinued.

sters, crossing the village street from Centre Family House to the Meeting House, were rmitted to enter the same door as Brethren, due to the relaxed rules in late 19th century.

Although the Shakers lived apart from the world in their social and religious habits, by no means were they oblivious to the customs and pleasures of the world. In almost childish fashion they enjoyed the special national and religious holidays. Thanksgiving was observed by a combination of religious and social services, and, like their Kentucky neighbors, they served a big feast. Perhaps more generously than other Kentuckians, they made gifts to the poor. The Christmas donation was practically mandatory. Benevolence to the poor was an integral part of Shaker faith.

Mother Ann's birthday was celebrated on February 29 or March 1. It was in most respects a second Christmas, representing the birth of the female Messiah. On this day the Believers read psalms, recited poetry, and engaged in dances.

Annually, in December, the Society set aside a day for purging the order of its sins, for reconciling the members one with another, and for silent prayer. There was no singing, dancing, or feasting. This was a day on which the members revealed their most disciplined natures.

It is difficult for persons used to the permissiveness of a worldly society to understand how so large a collection of human beings, of such a wide variation of ages, could carry out so successfully the rules of a celibate society. There is no doubt that the weaknesses of the flesh were prevalent at Pleasant Hill. Passions were perhaps as easily aroused there as anywhere else in Kentucky. For this reason manual labor, chanting, dancing and family "union meetings" were used to break the boredom and tedium of the daily celibate routine. Realizing a need for constant surveillance, the ruling elders were constantly on guard. Private unions under these circumstances were difficult, but not entirely impossible. Specific evidence of sexual irregularities is lacking in the earlier records. There were after 1880, according to journal entries, occasional elopements, and a few pregnancies. When such threats to the order of the Society occurred, there was consternation in the community as was often indicated by keepers of the family journals.

"Releasement" of the energies and human passions was

made occasionally by walks down to the Kentucky River and the Ferry Landing. The Shakers were captivated by the rugged gorge where the Dix River cuts its way through the great limestone barrier of the palisades to join the Kentucky. Below the cliffside road the little Cedar Run wound downhill over rock boulders and through a heavily wooded vale. In season, the Kentucky yielded catches of fish, and many of the Shaker Brethren participated in the sport of fishing.

Like most Americans, the Shakers loved to go on picnics and wagon rides. They would prepare food for a picnic and ride out to one of the out farms, or down to Brooklyn Bridge, or to Hickman Bridge (Camp Nelson), or to Nicholasville for a day's outing. These outings were occasions for viewing the world, buying sweetmeats from the stores along the way, and singing to the creaking of the wagons. On one occasion a dour scribe remarked that the "releasement" was a waste of time. To him it ranked with the frivolities of "going to a barbecue or Election." The communicants had, in the eyes of the scribe, behaved, "in such a manner as to disgrace . . . themselves, and (be) a scandal to the neighborhood."

Whatever internal or external criticism may have occurred concerning Shaker practices, it must be said that no other Kentuckians led such disciplined and orderly lives. With all the sternness and rigidity of puritanical New England, the joint focus of the Society was upon work and worship.

10 Proselyting

ONE OF THE greatest problems which the Shakers faced was that of keeping the membership of the families up to acceptable size. No doubt the ministry and elders hoped to expand the Society to rather large proportions, even to the planting of other communities in Kentucky, in addition to the ones at Pleasant Hill and South Union. The physical plan of the Pleasant Hill village indicates the ambitions of the Order in the formative age.

Changing times and human moods had an important bearing upon the fortunes of the Shaker communities. Pleasant Hill was formed in an age of deep religious agitation. Preachers of all faiths railed out against sin, and sex was the original sin. It is not surprising that some Kentucky frontiersmen could be proselyted into a celibate order. Too, there was a predominance of women and children in the Order, after 1828. Doubtless many females were proselyted because they looked upon communal living as an escape from boredom. Some of the female members may have found a certain amount of vicarious romantic appeal in the Society. The children had little or no choice.

In the area of utopian societies the Shaker community had its appeal. Whether individual members had clearly developed social and economic philosophies or not, they did sense a certain amount of group security at Pleasant Hill. The

Society removed its members from the hard competitiveness of the worldly community. It afforded a positive leadership in both temporal and spiritual affairs, and even relaxed many of the stern doctrines of the more fundamental religious teachings of Baptists, Methodists, Presbyterians, and Disciples of Christ.

A more productive source of new members for Pleasant Hill was the orphan left stranded. Recruiting orphans began about 1833. The Brethren who peddled garden seeds, brooms, and other Shaker products kept their eyes open for dependent children. In 1857, Micajah Burnett brought thirteen orphans home with him from New Orleans. Dr. John Shain, village physician and herb peddler, collected orphans on his travels.

Epidemics of deadly diseases which struck the West in the first half of the nineteenth century left crops of orphans; prime examples were the great outbreaks of cholera in 1833 and 1849. As time went on many public attitudes changed toward the question of adoption. State statutes were revised, and the Shakers possibly found it more difficult to bring large numbers of children into their Gathering Order. Three children brought into the Pleasant Hill Society, following the cholera epidemic of 1849, were the Pennebakers. These children grew to maturity in the Society and became pillars of community strength in the post-Civil War years.

The adoption of children placed a rather heavy responsibility on the Pleasant Hill Shakers. New recruits were assigned to the two families in the Gathering Order or to the Children's Order in the Church families where they came under the watchful supervision of caretakers. From the start they were separated by sexes and were drilled in the principles of Society discipline.

As lax as were Kentucky's early adoption laws, it was necessary for the Shakers to make sure each child was legally adopted. Otherwise they might have opened themselves to charges of kidnapping. Too, relatives of children or people of the community might establish claims to children after the Society had made heavy expenditures in their care, training, and education.

Shaker attitudes toward educational standards differed little from those of their rural Kentucky neighbors. Children were taught to read, to write, and to perform certain semi-skilled tasks. Classes were held from November to February during the dormant months on the farm. In 1835, Benjamin B. Dunlavy became the village's principal educator, but classes for girls were taught by the Sisters and boys were taught by the Brethren.

The curriculum consisted of elementary instruction in arithmetic, geography, reading, writing, and religion. For those who might help with herb gathering and preparation, instruction in elementary botany was made a part of their course of studies.

Sisters and children photographed at the Centre Family House with Professor William L. Linney, (right), state geologist, who had just lectured at the village.

Religious instruction consisted of reading the *New Testament*, the teachings of Mother Ann Lee, and Shaker history. In education, as in social and economic affairs, the Shakers lived separately from the world. Even so, they used some worldly textbooks, and even sought to inform themselves about modes of instruction in the Kentucky schools. They held to the philosophy in both religious and temporal instruction that teachers should not proceed beyond certain well-defined limits. In the years when there were approximately one hundred children at Pleasant Hill, sixty to seventy were enrolled in classes. The others were either too young or older than fifteen years.

Discipline was ever a challenge to the Shakers. Children, who were brought into the Society by parents, were generally separated from old family ties, and all old family relationships were broken. Some orphans often made individual if not unruly responses to Shaker discipline. The caretakers were obligated to make future and dedicated Shakers of the children. This was difficult to accomplish, and in many instances it was impossible. Occasionally there were runaways. Shaker Brethren often went into the countryside in search of their absconding charges. Some children knew the whereabouts of relatives and sought to establish themselves with members of their families. Relatives usually encouraged the children to run away, or they foiled Shakers searching for the runaways. Even though the Shakers had the law on their side, it was difficult to get it enforced in their favor. Too, the Shakers had great distaste for litigation. Generally speaking, if a member ran away once, he was lost to the Society. Even if he was returned to Pleasant Hill, he only ran away again.

There was the troublesome case of Caroline Whittymore whom the village scribe denominated the "Harlot of Harrodsburg." Caroline and her brother had been taken to Pleasant Hill when they were children. In the fall of 1846 she was driven out of the Society because of her "wicked ways." The scribe said she returned, "with one or two of her associated prostitutes under the influence of liquor," and asked to see her brother, James. Against orders she went to the East Wash

House and bore James off at the point of a horse pistol. James pleased the Believers by returning to Pleasant Hill in a few days. He, however, was an unusual case. When they were of an age to make a free choice scores of children left.

It was impossible for the Society of Believers to fill and maintain their ranks by proselyting. There were too many forces working against them. First, it was too great a strain for healthy and well-nourished men and women to live celibate lives in such close association. By no means did all of them bear the sexual frigidity and frustrations of Mother Ann Lee or of the older members of the Society at Pleasant Hill. Second, there was ever-present a strong materialistic tug at the normal selfish natures of the members. Third, the impact of an expanding and changing America on the Shakers was great. Individual members did not remain oblivious to what was happening about them. The Shakers themselves estimated they only retained ten percent of their young.

The scribes often lamented in the journals that a Brethren or a Sister had departed. Adults stole away secretly and no doubt with a guilty conscience. To desert the pure gospel was to embrace eternal damnation. Often when a Believer departed his name was entered in the *Family Temporal Journal* as a "puff of trash has blown away," "worthless scamp," "dead limbs will drop off," or "So the Devil has got you at last, you good-for-nothing."

Whatever the cause for desertions or the epithets cast after the apostatizers, the highly disturbing fact was that after 1845 the Shakers received almost no dependable adult members. Anxiety about receiving new members left the Society open to willful exploitation by people who came into the Order during the bad winter months and departed in the spring, or by those who sought only temporary surcease from the overwhelming cares of the "world."

The "world" was not always as kind a place as the adult deserters imagined it. If they had been at Pleasant Hill for any length of time and had lived by the regimen of the Society, they found it difficult to adjust to the more casual tenor of worldly life. Worldly neighbors found the ex-Shakers peculiar in their habits and were not always hospitable to them. Occasionally a father or mother departed the Society and left a family behind. Even though they had forsworn Shaker family fellowship, they were back in a short time seeking readmission.

Readmission to the Shaker Society was possible where members went out into the world for a brief fling. Sometimes these worldly adventures resulted in the future stabilization of a member. As desperate as the Society was for adult members, it could hardly afford to be other than generous toward repentant members who sought readmission. On the other hand the Society expelled members, usually for moral indiscretions, and then refused to readmit them.

After the Civil War the problems of securing and holding new members were well-nigh insurmountable even though discipline of the Order was greatly relaxed, and the name and teachings of Mother Ann were no longer revered in the old ways. The visiting Eldress, Harriett Bullard, was to write of the Pleasant Hill Shakers in 1889, "The world and the Believers seemingly walk hand in hand. They admit adults and children from the surrounding neighborhood . . . They learn from Sabbath papers gotten up outside which teach a false theology that is easier to implant in the young minds than it will be to uproot in years to come. And their songs are threaded thro and thro with the old orthodox religion."

In other areas discipline broke down or was unknown after the Civil War. A crippled boy attacked Benjamin B. Dunlavy with his crutches. There were charges in 1872 of malicious cutting with intent to kill, and two boys attempted to settle a dispute with pistols. Life at Pleasant Hill had other thorns; the moral behavior of converts deteriorated. No doubt the Society's scribe was right in referring to transient members as "worthless scamps." Henry Daily summed up the weaknesses of the efforts to find new members when he wrote, "we have men here with us who lye in Bed till within a few minutes of breakfast time and yet our head people let them do so with impunity instead of driving them off as they should do."

11 Wayfarers

SOME OF THE early converts who moved to Pleasant Hill brought their slaves with them. Officially, the Shakers took no public position toward slavery; actually they were passionately anti-slavery. They did, however, reflect an anti-slavery feeling in their village journals describing it as an unjustifiable institution which belonged to the world. There were never more than six or eight Negro members of the Society. Negroes were accepted on equal terms in order of worship; and one Negro member was appointed to serve as a kitchen deaconess.

Other Negroes were employed as laborers on the farm. These were mostly slaves of neighboring farmers. Some became Shaker converts. In 1859, the Believers purchased Jonas Crutcher, a Believer for nineteen years. A few slaves were purchased and emancipated to prevent their being sold South to cotton and sugar plantation owners.

The Shakers were most humane people. The slave, the wayfarer, the victim of disaster, the unfortunate in general found them ready to share their goods and roof. Located as it was on the road between Lexington and Harrodsburg, the village was a good day's travel from the former city and a good stopping place on the way from the latter. Until 1836, the Society operated a public tavern for visitors. The Believers were generous people and perhaps were too free with their hospitality for their tavern to yield a profit. It was recorded that tavern-keeping was discontinued as being "incompatible with the calling and order of Believers except so far as the principles of charity and hospitality might require."

There is no way of knowing how much free food the Shakers distributed over the years to tramps and beggars who came to the village. For three-quarters of a century there were literally hundreds of transients of one sort or another who passed through Pleasant Hill. Most offensive were those individuals who, after the Civil War, moved in and out of the village at will. To the Shakers these were known as "turnbacks." One such bum was Henry Scales. Deacon Henry Daily wrote that he was "too lazy and trifling to earn an honest living, and that he had the crust to impose himself" upon the Shakers.

Pleasant Hill on many occasions displeased other Shaker communities by its official laxness in enforcing the rules of the faith. In the latter years the ministry in Kentucky accepted into the Pleasant Hill community Shakers who had departed other communities. One such drifter was George Beggs, who moved back and forth between Whitewater, Ohio, and Pleasant Hill. Beggs was not only a wanderer, he was a murderer who had served time in the penitentiary for killing a Negro. At Pleasant Hill he stole six hundred dollars from Elder Andrew Bloomberg and went to Burgin where he got drunk.

The cold months of winter brought their crop of cold weather converts who found the community ritual endurable until the warm days of spring when they went out into the world again. "Winter Shakers" were no doubt spongers of the first order. In 1882, Henry Daily lamented, "We have just finished filling up the Centre House with men, that is, Winter Shakers. Our table is full and running over," and "we may expect to have anything to live on and yet take in every family that comes along. They go at loose ends, do just as they please and say what they choose . . . not pay half their board all winter then leave in the spring with all we have in clothing and food . . . leave us to work all summer."

In 1848, the Shakers became interested in another religious communal sect. A group of Swedish dissenters, the Jansonites, immigrated to the community of Bishop Hill in Henry County near Galesburg, Illinois. Like many communal sects of this period, the faithful were brought together by their belief in a self-annointed Messiah. In this case it was Eric Janson who claimed to be the vicar of Christ on earth. He subscribed to a pietistic doctrine that looked to the perfectability of man on earth and a foreseeable day of millennial happiness.

Man's perfection was man's sole objective on earth, and, to make him worthy, Eric Janson proposed that men should separate themselves from the corrupting influences of worldly neighbors. At Bishop Hill he gathered his flock about him in a theocratic community similar to those of George Rapp at New Harmony, Indiana, and in Economy and Harmony in Pennsylvania. By 1848, there were approximately

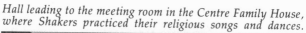

Hall leading to the meeting room in the Centre Family House, where Shakers practiced their religious songs and dances.

800 Jansonites in Illinois.

Benjamin B. Dunlavy and the deacons of Pleasant Hill became interested in Janson's community, after two travelers had come to Pleasant Hill in April 1848 to view Shaker activities. The Shakers saw in it many points of similarity and opened communication with them. The Kentuckians contributed improved breeding stock to build up the Swedes' herds and flocks. They gave their new neighbors instructions in dyeing of wool and improved methods of weaving. They also shared their knowledge of fruit and vegetable growing. In turn, the Swedes built wagons for use at Pleasant Hill.

Inevitably, the two communities communicated on religious matters. When, in 1855, Nils Heden visited Kentucky to see firsthand the working of the Shaker community, he was impressed by life in the village and by the noncompetitiveness of the Society. Too, he accepted the doctrine of celibacy as being also sanctioned by God and brought about the adoption of the practice at Bishop Hill.

No better opening had presented itself for the proselyting of new members than the Swedish community. Benjamin B. Dunlavy and George Runyon went to Bishop Hill in 1855 as missionaries. They preached the sanctity of a female Messiah, and the doctrine of celibacy. They were rewarded for their efforts by the conversion of Andrew Bloomberg and his family. In turn Bloomberg became a missionary and in time was to bring many converts to Pleasant Hill.

Between 1855 and 1858 a considerable number of Janson's flock came to Kentucky. Many of them had become alienated from the Bishop Hill community because of arbitrary actions by Eric Janson. Among the Swedish converts was Ann Sophia Janson, widow of Eric Janson, who proved to be a useful interpreter for her people. In a short time, however, she became disenchanted and returned to Illinois. With the disaffection of Sister Janson began the departure of the Swedes. They left as they came by "ones and twos." In time the Pleasant Hill scribe lamented that the Swedes had proved disappointing. "Swedish blood," he wrote, "is as much opposed to the Cross as any other." This experience, however, formed the groundwork for a post-Civil War mission to Sweden.

Nothing proved the fallacy of the Shaker doctrine more than failure to recruit new members, and most important of all, new leadership. The anxiety of the ministry at Pleasant Hill to recruit new members often led it to overextend the hospitality of the community at home and to contribute too generously to an unappreciative outside world.

The Shakers proved too naive to deal with changing economic and social conditions in an ever-expanding America after the Civil War. As American society matured, it produced an ever-increasing amount of human dross which was not at all adverse to accepting an excessive amount of free hospitality no matter what theological tag was tied to it.

As the Society lost members and the remaining members grew older, it became ever more difficult for the Shakers to sustain their former high level of production. The elders and ministers grew too senile to administer the policies of the Society, and, as Elder Daily said, they allowed themselves and their community to be shamefully abused by bums and rascals who beset them after 1865 and who had no regard for their religious or social beliefs. All the other Shaker Societies experienced the same sort of decline.

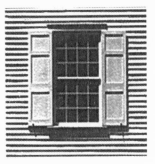

12   In the Tempest of War

THE BASIS OF Shaker religious ethics was kindness and
peace, a philosophy derived from the Quakers. Although
tucked away in the midst of their large, landed domain, the
Believers were not insured from the conflicts of the world
about them. Twice in their history they had seen Kentucky
become involved in war; once in 1812, and later in the Mexican War. In the golden decade, 1850-1860, when the colony
prospered and the religious Order was safely under the control of the elders, there was the uneasy feeling of impending
sectional conflict in the Nation.

Both the Shakers and their Kentucky neighbors were
caught in the midst of these sectional disputes, and both
desired peace. The opening of the decade had seen Henry
Clay attempt to achieve a compromise of key issues, and at
the close of the decade, his successor, John Jordan Crittenden, had sought to devise a formula which would keep the
peace.

The Kentucky scene had been disturbed by the bloody
election riot in Louisville on August 6, 1855, as much a man-
ifestation of the breaking of the old political ties as it was an
outbreak of militant nationalism. Shakers were opposed to
slavery without being militant abolitionists. In this attitude
they found support among an ever-growing Kentucky
yeomanry. Over the years they were made conscious of the

evils of slavery by what they observed in the neighboring slave sales in Lexington and Harrodsburg and by the acts of some slave owners on adjoining farms. Most of all, they were conscious of slavery as an active political force in the State. They had witnessed the struggle over the Kentucky Constitution in 1849 and were aware of the growing tensions in each succeeding election in the 1850s.

Nevertheless, Kentucky was to have one of its most prosperous decades just prior to the Civil War. Because of its location in the keystone position of the Ohio borderland, war was a dire threat to its well-being. The Kentucky newspapers of the period were filled with stories of political contention and sectional conflict. The Shakers were not oblivious to this fact, nor were they uninformed of the results of the election of 1860. Their journals and letters all reflect the concern of the elders at Pleasant Hill. One of the greatest threats to the well-being of the Society was the possibility of Kentucky's becoming a battleground in a civil war. The ministry gave ample evidence of having knowledge of the forces which divided sentiment in the State.

The Shakers stood to lose heavily by war because the southern market for their products would be destroyed. Over the years the expanding cotton belt had been a highly profitable trading area, and the Shakers had been successful in exploiting it without having to become emotionally involved in the slavery issue. This was a difficult position because they were fundamentally committed to the Union.

In the campaign of 1860 the political scene was drawn to the very door of Pleasant Hill. In August of that year, 18,000 Kentuckians assembled at the northern end of the projected High Bridge across the Kentucky River to hear speeches in behalf of the Constitutional Unionists, John Bell and Edward Everett. It was a grand occasion in which the speakers stressed the importance of preserving the Union—slavery or no slavery. Later some of the Pleasant Hill elders went to Harrodsburg to hear John Jordan Crittenden speak in behalf of his proposed resolutions. All of the pro-Unionist speakers impressed the Shakers. Deacon James Ballance, who was not present at the meeting, wrote, "I believe they (pro-Secessionists) can shew no reason for destroying this blessed Union." Then he observed, "Only that a majority of its people has sought proper to elect Abraham Lincoln for President of these United States, that is, saying the minority must rule or in other words the people cannot govern themselves, and of course they must have a monarch placed over them to keep them in subject." War was unthinkable.

Following the election in November 1860, it became apparent at once that the Union of States would be broken by the secession of South Carolina followed by other slave states. Kentucky was thrown into turmoil. By the opening of the new year it was clear the Crittenden Compromise would be rejected, as would the proposals for the meeting of peace or conciliatory conventions to undertake restoration of the Union. Both in Louisville and Frankfort frantic efforts were being made to keep Kentucky out of the impending conflict. These moves resulted in declaring the Commonwealth to be in a state of armed neutrality.

On the other side of the issue, pro-Secessionists were active in their efforts to take Kentucky into the Confederacy. By summer 1861, the Kentucky State Guard was preparing to march south and join the Confederate Army. In August this body held a muster in the village street of Pleasant Hill, an omen of things to come for that peaceful island. One of the village chroniclers looked on this noisy demonstration with horror. To him the cocky young guardsmen were learning "the most successful method of letting out the heart's blood of their opponent—and for what?" To him it was "the most singular and sad spectacle ever witnessed since creation . . . to see people possessing the best government ever vouchsafed by heaven to mortals on earth, commanding the admiration of the world, exhibiting unparalleled prosperity, peace and happiness . . . a refuge for the oppressed of all nations—and then to rise up without any cause, except disappointed ambitions, rivalry and jealousy, and to go fighting like dogs and butchering and murdering each other, and glorying in their deeds of blood like demons. And yet they claim to be true Christians." Perhaps no more eloquent observation was made in Kentucky on the State's involvement in the approaching war.

John Hunt Morgan and the State Guards went south. Simon Bolivar Buckner and Albert Sidney Johnson had come home to organize Kentuckians into Confederate regiments. Nearby, across the sweeping valleys of the Dix and Kentucky Rivers, Camp Dick Robinson was organized to enlist men to protect Kentucky. Wagons brought over from Lexington the shipment of "Lincoln guns" which had been sent to Kentucky by the War Department. A few young Shakers went over to the new camp and enlisted in the name of keeping the peace. The elders, however, brought them back to Pleasant Hill.

By September 1861, Kentucky was drawn into the war. General Leonidas Polk had invaded the state as far as Columbus on the Mississippi River, and quickly Buckner had concentrated forces at Bowling Green. In southeastern Kentucky the battles of Wildcat and Mills Springs were fought. War was now a reality, and again the Shakers were faced with the possibility of being drafted. A petition praying that they not be involved in a draft to do military service was sent to Frankfort.

Though they sat on their island of peace and tranquility south of the Kentucky River, there was the ominous threat that sooner or later the War in fact would come, like the martial Home Guards, to their door. Shaker trade was brought almost to a standstill, and the Believers had no other choice but to await the turn of events. In July 1862, General John Hunt Morgan and 816 cavalry-infantrymen dashed across the southern Kentucky border, and at Tompkinsville struck the 3rd Pennsylvania Cavalry a crushing blow. They then roared across southeastern Kentucky frightening the inhabitants of Bear Wallow, New Hope, Lebanon, Springfield and Harrodsburg. On August 13, the furious raider and his men stormed through Harrodsburg headed toward the Kentucky River.

Again Pleasant Hill was in the path of armed forces.

Rumors preceded Morgan, and the West Family deacon predicted all sorts of dire consequences. Morgan's men would burn the village, steal the horses, rob the stores. Horses were driven off and hidden, and other protective measures were taken. Fortunately the raiders only ate a hearty meal in the village and passed on without further disturbing the Shakers. There were, however, other raids to come.

Following defeat at Shiloh, Confederate forces in Tennessee made an attempt to turn the tide of campaigning back to Kentucky. Late in August 1862, General Manson and the advance forces of General Kirby-Smith's command attacked General William Nelson's command near Kingston and drove the Federal forces back in a running fight to the Clay's Ferry Bridge. On September 1, the Confederates had occupied Lexington. This action was fairly well-removed from Pleasant Hill, nevertheless the Shakers were to experience the woes of

Frame building, in use as the post office, and located on the main stage route between Lexington and Harrodsburg, pictured in late 19th century photograph.

conflict in the next two months resulting from this invasion.

While Kirby-Smith occupied Lexington, General Braxton Bragg entered Kentucky south of Bowling Green and began a hurried march northward. He advanced under the surveillance of General Don Carlos Buell and his Union forces in Louisville. Instead of striking at Louisville, Bragg turned inland toward Springfield and Lebanon and then toward Danville and Harrodsburg by way of the rural village of Perryville.

All of this activity caused a heavy movement of troops in and around Pleasant Hill. Captain William C. P. Breckinridge and a hundred of his men arrived in the village at dusk one evening in search of food and horses. Elder Rufus Bryant refused Captain Breckinridge's request for horses and the main body of the command passed on. Stragglers, however, returned to harass the elder. They held a pistol to his head and threatened to take him to Lexington if he did not comply.

A village scribe wrote, "They presented their pistols, threatening he should be taken double quick to Lexington if they were not produced." The stubborn Bryant held out against them. Then they turned on him but he was so gentle and passive the Confederates gave up. They searched the barns but found no horses. The most the ruffians got was a subduing and some food.

Other hungry troops galloped up to be fed prior to the bloody battle at Perryville on October 8. Among these visitors were Captain J. C. Alexander of Harrodsburg and eighty-eight troops. In time, Pleasant Hill was to become an unwilling commissary for Confederate troops. Deacon James Ballance said the Confederates were starving in their own land, and "took this State to get something to eat."

Both Braxton Bragg and Kirby-Smith sought diligently to restock Confederate stores from the rich stores of materials in Central Kentucky. They gathered so many goods they ran out of wagons with which to transport their loot. On September 24, the Confederate quartermaster in Lexington requisitioned light, stout Shaker wagons to be delivered to that place. Seven were sent, but the Shakers begged that they be allowed to keep the seventh. The Confederates paid six hundred eighty dollars in Confederate script for the wagons, but, as Deacon Ballance observed, this was "worthless trash."

While General Bragg vacillated in Central Kentucky trying to install Richard Hanes as Confederate governor in Frankfort, Kirby-Smith moved fifteen hundred troops to Harrodsburg. This move added woe indeed to the Shakers' lives. The routine at Pleasant Hill was seriously disrupted. Benjamin Dunlavy wrote, the "horses, wagons, stock, flour, preserves, cloth, etc." were hidden. Even unripe fruit was plucked from the trees to prevent its loss. Religious services were out of the question.

On October 5, the first concentration of Kirby-Smith's forces arrived at Pleasant Hill. They were hungry and inconsiderate. James Ballance described these troops as, "ragged, greasy and dirty and some barefoot, looked more like bipeds of pandemonium than beings of this earth or the angels of deliverance from Lincoln's bondage."

While the Confederate horde was hungry, it was even thirstier. Late September and early October 1862 was an exceedingly dry season. When the troops reached Pleasant Hill they rushed to the pumps in the yards, "like herds of buffalo at a salt lick and thronged the kitchen doors and windows like flocks of hungry wolves and devoured the bread, meat and pies etc., that were distributed to them with the greediness of half-starved dogs." The East Family chronicler said, "some even threatened to shoot others if they did not divide with them."

It is not hard to imagine how anguished the Shakers were over this greedy, riotous scene. To them it was enough to melt the hardest heart, to see "grown men, dirty and ragged, armed with deadly weapons and begging at our doors as if they were famishing with hunger and thirst." It was but the beginning. For the next few days the faithful were forced to feed as many as a thousand troops a day.

Confusion for the inhabitants was made even greater at Pleasant Hill by the fact that General Humphrey Marshall's command was ordered back toward Lexington to guard the intersection of the Versailles and Harrodsburg Pikes. In Benjamin Dunlavy's opinion, "The Army seemed to be in perfect consternation, marching and counter-marching with as much uneasiness as a troop of ants on a firebrand." This horde exhausted the Brethren and Sisters, who often worked until after midnight to feed their uninvited guests.

At the out-of-the-way area on the rim of the Chaplin Hills above Perryville the two armies stumbled into battle. Dunlavy wrote that the battle was "said by knowing ones to have been the severest and most fatal battle of the War, considering the numbers and length of time they were engaged." The roar of cannon could be heard at Pleasant Hill. They belched "forth slaughter and death . . . and the Union forces and rebels are slaughtering up one another at a killing rate." Men who had stood and begged so greedily at the family lot pumps and at the kitchen doors and windows were now lying dispatched to eternity.

Once again hordes of straggling troops in retreat were to descend upon the Shaker village. Troops dropping back through Harrodsburg toward Lexington came to stand once again at kitchen doors and windows. This time they had the stain of battle and death on them. A table was set up in the Trustees' Office yard and kept filled with food. On October 11, ten thousand troops passed through Pleasant Hill. The village was converged upon by Confederates and the Shakers fed approximately fourteen hundred troops that day.

On the twelfth, Colonel Richard Gano stopped for breakfast with three hundred troops and all that day stragglers from Perryville came by to be fed. It is little wonder that a Sister observed, "after all this war-like commotion the ensuing night was as calm as the valley of death; and the rising moon shed a silvery light over this Pleasant Hill of Zion, as soft—as Milton's night in the paradise of our first parents."

By middle October the Shakers could take stock of their experiences with the Confederates, whose cause they detested. They were intimidated into extending their hospitality. Although they fed only a small portion of the troops, the Shakers estimated they served eight to nine thousand meals.

Even though the gentle people of Pleasant Hill were greatly imposed upon by the Confederate troops, it was a remarkable fact that they suffered almost no loss or damage of communal property. Only 700 fence rails were burned at camp fires. The Shakers supplied 1,350 bushels of corn for forage, 9 horses were stolen, 6 wagons were commandeered, and four or five hundred dollars worth of preserves were exchanged for Confederate money. The Sisters cared for some of the wounded, one of them, a Georgian, died and was buried in the Shaker graveyard. Brethren took wagonloads of food and sanitary supplies to treat the wounded at Perryville and Harrodsburg.

Although the Battle of Perryville drew the war once again away from Kentucky, Pleasant Hill was still exposed to both military and guerrilla harassment. In November 1863, Federal troops fearing another Morgan raid sank the boats at the Shaker Ferry. It was necessary for the Shakers to post sentinels to watch out for approaching troops in order to hide their horses from thieves.

During 1864, there was grave fear of the guerrilla raids which beset all Kentucky. The Shakers were not to be disappointed. On the night of October 7, "one arm" Sam Berry, a seceder who had been raised at Pleasant Hill, robbed the mail stage at Shawnee Run, and then robbed Elhanon W. Scott, Henry Daily, and some Sisters who happened to be passing the scene on their way from Harrodsburg. The Shakers lost a watch, some money and two good horses to their former convert. On October 19, guerrillas again stole clothing in a raid, and in the following April they looted the Post Office.

For the Shakers, as for so many Americans, the Civil War was a great dividing period. The Society lost membership, and a spirit of insubordination showed itself. Economically, the War all but closed the channels of trade which had yielded the Society an income in years past. As Amos Ballance wrote, "the spirit and feeling—seems to have left this part of the world."

13   In the Seed of Time

LIKE EVERY other institution in Kentucky, the Society of Believers experienced a period of change following the Civil War. Changes which came to Pleasant Hill were due largely to failures of Fourierism abroad; to abandonment of the idea of a Utopia in the United States after the Civil War; and to internal failures within the Society to prepare for those years in which inevitable demands would be made for younger and imaginative leadership. Inside Pleasant Hill, members were growing old, and there were no young replacements for them. One of the miracles of Pleasant Hill, as well as of the whole Shaker movement, is that it succeeded so well for so long. Apparently three strong elements contributed to this success. The first was dedication to a central spiritual idea in which they believed men could achieve perfectibility in a well-ordered society. Second, the Shakers started from a solid middle or lower class yeomanry who placed more emphasis on the virtue of hard work than upon personal pride, comfort, and vanity. Third, the Shakers generally had dedicated and hard-headed administration. For the Shakers, life itself was not a sinful ordeal, but rather one in which a leisurely but steady pace of occupation and recreation was to be desired. The America which came out of the Civil War was too crass and materialistic for a community of gentle rural folk to thrive in the old way. Machines elsewhere in America produced furniture, brooms, preserves, and all the other things produced on the Pleasant Hill farm and in the shops. The standardized processes of commodity production, for instance, reduced prices on food items below the level that the Shakers could make profits.

The new machines of the post-war years and the expansion of the great northwestern and western grain belt offered enormous competition to the old fashioned mill at Pleasant Hill. The raising of fine cattle was the only Shaker industry left largely untouched by the times, and even the great western cattle drives had some bearing on it. New transportation facilities changed greatly in the old Shaker market areas. The Lower South was caught up in a seige of biting poverty, and became a region where merchants from Louisville, St. Louis, Cincinnati, and Baltimore competed actively for markets for cheap goods. If the former slaveholder in the South had his problems with reconstruction, the Shakers themselves felt the sting of the New Order. Although few Negroes were associated with the Pleasant Hill Society, there were many Negro hired hands on the farms, first as neighboring slaves, then as freedmen. Throughout, the Shakers had made no racial distinction in their attitudes. In September 1869, a note was found on the Post Office door threatening dire consequences to the Order if it continued its tolerant racial policies.

There were strong indications that the anti-freedman warning came from the Ku Klux Klan. As it turned out the culprit was a Shaker tenant. Occasionally the Klan did admonish a Shaker hired hand to move on. In 1873, an attempt was made, supposedly by the Ku Klux Klan, to blackmail the Society into sending two hundred dollars to a E. J. Rees of Oxford, Ohio, to prevent the village from being destroyed by fire.

There were many other outside irritations which disturbed the tenor of Shaker life after 1865. The enormous pressure of the "outside world" bore constantly on the elders, and they were now scarcely capable of dealing effectively, as the Shakers once did, with external affairs. A lack of young and aggressive leaders was the most serious challenge.

Two prominent Pleasant Hill leaders, Sister Jane Sutton and elderly Trustee John Rufus Bryant, Jr., shown about 1870, on stoop of East Family House.

The Pleasant Hill elders had grown old and weary. It became necessary in 1868 to relieve Eldress Sarah Jenkins of her administrative responsibilities. James Rankin remained as First Elder, but he was an aged man. The Pleasant Hill ministry was reduced by one in number. An attempt was made to use a single ministry to administer both the Pleasant Hill and South Union villages in order to bolster the strength of this body. The plan quickly proved unsatisfactory.

An enormously important change took place when the aged and paralytic Rufus Bryant was relieved of his duties as trustee in 1872. Elhanon Scott and Benjamin Dunlavy were put in his place. Dunlavy had advanced through the ranks of the eldership of the First Order of the Church, but his interests had been more theological and philosophical than practical. He assumed leadership in 1874, when James Rankin was reduced to Second Elder, and when the Society needed the most astute financial management. In this move the Shakers had violated a central policy by combining the posts of temporal and spiritual leadership. In time Dunlavy was to make disastrous financial commitments, which all but bankrupted the Society in the end.

Proselyting for new members had proved a failure. The Society had failed in all of its efforts to feed into the Order the vigorous young membership which could perform the labor necessary to keep the vast farm and family organization in prosperous operation. Too, the religious service lacked the vigor and spontaneity which came from youth. In this period only two young men offered promise of vigorous leadership; they were William and Francis Pennebaker of the West Family. William was educated as a doctor and Francis as a dentist. While in medical school, William was subjected to the changing philosophies of the age, and he brought home to Pleasant Hill a more progressive point of view than had characterized the "gospel order" in the past. The Pennebakers, however, became disruptive personalities because of their inflexibility in dealing with current crises.

The failure to feed into the system youthful leadership confronted the Shakers with almost insoluble problems.

Their failure to find sufficient sources of income to meet operating expenses was equally great. By 1880, all of the old trade outlets were practically closed by ruinous commercial competition. No longer could their salesmen find buyers for their products. Even the basis of Kentucky farming itself was undergoing rapid changes. Fields once planted in hemp were now growing the newly-developed burley tobacco. In these later years the beginnings of the cigarette industry in North Carolina would vastly influence the Kentucky economy. For religious reasons the Shakers could not capitalize on this new crop. Livestock was still profitable, but the Shakers now lacked the astute management necessary to turn profits from their herds, despite the fact that their animals still took prizes in the neighboring county fairs.

Disaster stalked the faltering Pleasant Hill community. In 1873, a cow barn burned, the work of a Swedish convert recently arrived from Sweden. Three years later the Centre Family's huge barn, shops, and outbuildings were burned in what was to be the village's most serious fire. All of these fires were acts of arsonists and were total losses because the Society had no insurance.

Almost as disastrous as the fires was the fact that the Swedish experiment to recruit new members had resulted in the loss of precious funds and the addition of few permanent members. The Swedish mission was the biggest proselyting effort undertaken by the Pleasant Hill Shakers. Thus the hard times of the 1870s pressed excessively upon the Shakers. Benjamin Dunlavy was incapable of meeting the challenges of the age. He and his associates violated the strict admonitions against contracting debts. By 1880, the rich landholdings of the Society were encumbered in forty thousand dollars of debt without foreseeable opportunities to pay the debt.

Dunlavy and his fellow elders were caught in another squeeze. They became involved in internal arguments between those who wished to live by the strict rules of Mother Ann and those progressives who wished to liberalize church procedures and to make significant changes in the whole "gospel order." The latter argued that to follow such a procedure would result in the recruitment of new members. This was only one point. Beginning with 1868, the Pleasant Hill residents went to the polls, a sign they could no longer ignore the changing world about them. A scribe for the Centre Family wrote, "The brethren that were of lawful age went to Harrodsburg and voted for the County to subscribe $300,000 dollars for building a Rail Road from Louisville via of Harrodsburg to Virginia. This is the first time in the history of this society that the brethren have voted on any public measure." They realized that a vote not cast would be as a vote against the measure, and the success of the issue would be beneficial to the Shakers.

In many other ways the affairs of the world flowed into Pleasant Hill. An organ was purchased in 1874 to be used in giving singing lessons. Outside musicians in time came to the family meeting rooms to give concerts. To the chronicler, Henry Daily, this marked the beginning of the end. A significant departure from the old order was the acceptance of public money to sustain the village school.

If the world flowed into Pleasant Hill, the Shakers went out as well to meet it. They were excited by events which

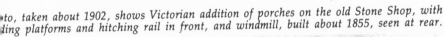

to, taken about 1902, shows Victorian addition of porches on the old Stone Shop, with ding platforms and hitching rail in front, and windmill, built about 1855, seen at rear.

occurred about them. When the Cincinnati, New Orleans & Texas Pacific Railway built its line between Cincinnati and Chattanooga, one of the main engineering challenges was the building of High Bridge at the Shaker Ferry just below the confluence of the Kentucky and Dix Rivers. A 240-foot high structure, it was an exciting accomplishment which the Shakers watched with great interest. When President Rutherford B. Hayes and General William T. Sherman came to dedicate the bridge on September 12, 1879, the residents of Pleasant Hill were there to greet them.

The coming of the railroad largely destroyed the significance of the old Shaker Landing, and it also went far toward destroying their isolation from the world. Now that the Shakers had little if any further business dealings in the South, they had nearby railway connections to the region. High Bridge and its dramatically beautiful river gorge setting became a popular excursion spot. As a result the Shakers took in boarders and ran a regular taxi service to the Ferry and up the opposite shoulder of the palisades to the north end of the bridge.

Again the impracticality of Shaker management was to turn a promising idea into a questionable asset. The Trustees' Office was turned into a boardinghouse where visitors could secure meals for forty or fifty cents. A license was secured to sell tobacco, and Pleasant Hill began to resemble a resort. It became almost impossible to maintain the old Shaker Order with so many strangers about. Even the religious ceremonies were neglected in order to serve the boarders.

This was not the only distraction. The High Bridge Association rented land from the Shakers on which to create a camp meeting ground. The Shakers secured the concession to operate the dining and stable facilties. The camp meeting with its emotional evangelistic preaching and crowd excitement became a garden of temptation. Sometimes upwards of twelve thousand persons gathered there to hear a fiery evangelist like Sam Jones lambast sin and the devil. Tempted Shakers attended the meetings, forgetting their own services.

The great dances and spiritual exercises of the Sabbath

Meetings deteriorated into little more than perfunctory services. As a matter of fact, services were held largely in the
family houses and the old weekly meetings in the Meeting
House were bypassed. So far had the order of the religious
meetings degenerated that Protestant ministers preached in
the services, and Believers attended the services of neighboring churches. By 1887, the Pleasant Hill Society was holding a
joint Sunday School for Believers and worldly attendants.
Village scribes viewed these practices with awe. There was
every sign that the Shakers were losing their sense of discipline, and nothing but a miracle of new leadership, and
increased young membership, and new sources of revenue
would help renew the rigid community standards of earlier
years.

Since its beginning, inhabitants of Pleasant Hill were
scrupulously honest. Both religious discipline and common
ownership of property had reduced selfishness and greed to a
minimum. In the declining years, however, not only arson
but also thievery plagued the Society. Thieves rifled fruit and
storage cellars, cribs, and other storage places. These thieves
turned out to be members of the community. As an example,
when the Centre Family gardener died two hundred fifty
dollars was found hidden in the farm shop. Even the second
elder of the East Family was expelled for embezzling family
funds. In the sale of produce from the farm, it was discovered
that deacons and farmhands alike had been selling produce
and pocketing the money.

Benjamin Dunlavy was incapable of exercising stern discipline over his charges. He was vacillating, lenient, and no
doubt unaware of some of the forces of deterioration which
had set in. Within the Society there was a conflict of ideas.
William Pennebaker advocated closer ties with the world,
and perhaps a more liberal form of Christianity. He also
sought to develop more individual enterprise among the
families. These views brought him into conflict, not only
with Elder Dunlavy, but also with the visiting ministry of
New Lebanon. Pennebaker, in 1878, led the West Family out
of the joint support of the Church. Ten days later the East

Family withdrew.

This division among the families meant the beginning of the end for Pleasant Hill as a unified religious community. Lands, livestock, shops, farm implements, and all other properties were divided. Labor could no longer be performed in the same way as in the past. Members had grown too old to perform heavy or confining tasks.

Membership dropped to a disastrously low figure. In 1884, the West Lot Family had only eleven members and was disbanded. The entire village population had dropped well below two hundred with the division of the families. Effective administration of the Society on the basic plan of communal living now became an impossibility. Beset by worries and frustrations, and perhaps, some sense of guilt over his incapable management, Benjamin Dunlavy died at age eighty-one on August 17, 1886. Shakers from South Union and Union Village, and those of Pleasant Hill were joined by neighbors from the world to give him the last big Shaker funeral. Earlier, however, Shaker burials were modest and dignified affairs. The spirits, howling over the old graveyard as Shaker spirits might have done, and Mother Ann, herself, must have had some pointed questions to ask Elder Benjamin about his stewardship.

The mourners had scarcely returned from the graveyard before they discovered that financial disaster awaited them. Elder Dunlavy had subscribed to two hundred fifty shares of Nevada gold mining stock, now worthless. A man named Oliver Watson in Virginia held a note signed by Dunlavy, which with accrued interest, amounted to fourteen thousand dollars. No record of the Society showed any trace of the transaction. In the court litigation which followed, it was discovered that Dunlavy had signed a note made to a Madison M. Mays of Waynesburg, Ohio, probably on the belief he was securing a loan from the Zoarites of Ohio, or the Economites of Pennsylvania.

Elder Dunlavy sought the loan with the hope of resuscitating the revenue of Pleasant Hill. Francis Pennebaker had invented a farm utility wagon which had high rear wheels and very low wheels in front. A box mounted on a frame could be shifted back and forth by use of ropes and pulleys, and could be dumped with ease by the driver from his seat. The low front wheels permitted short turns. It was patented by the Pennebaker brothers. Models of this wagon were actually built and demonstrated, but the Shakers were unable to manufacture it cheaply enough to be sold competitively.

The second project which Dunlavy hoped would succeed was the processing of an aromatic elixir of malt. The idea had been sold to the Shakers by Sarah Rupe and a mountebank Indiana doctor named T. K. Hardman. The catch was that Rupe and Hardman sold four digester machines and the rights for the sale of malt in Jefferson, Fayette, Jessamine, and Mercer Counties. At first the malt did enjoy a favorable sale, but it failed to maintain its market.

The Watson case was decided against the Shakers in 1896, even though the Kentucky judges personally recognized that the Society may have been an innocent victim. In the face of the law the judges had no other choice. The Court's judgment involved the already poverty-strickened Society in

rn of the century antique picture post card shows visitors on a tour to see the village of ¿asant Hill, which had become, by then, an object of curiosity and relic of the past.

twenty thousand dollars additional debts. There was now no choice but to mortgage some of the lands. The Louisville Title Company advanced thirty thousand dollars on 3,334 acres.

In 1896, there were fewer than sixty Shakers left, and most of these were elderly people. A. M. Barkley of Lexington opened a hotel in the East Family House, and Sister Jane Sutton was placed in charge. That year General John B. Castleman of Louisville bought 766 acres of Shaker land and the Trustees' Office for slightly more than twenty-seven dollars an acre.

Pleasant Hill had fallen into decay. There were no further hopes that either it or its Shaker faith could be restored. The dwindling ranks of elderly Shakers who lingered behind were only awaiting the moment when they too would join the spirits of the past. The past century had known its moments of triumph, but now Elder Rufus Bryant's great meadows no longer produced prize-winning cattle and sheep. The shops were rotting, and the crafts of the Shakers were now forgotten. The world itself flowed over the village. Even on the northern bank of the Kentucky River the annual evangelical revivals all but drowned out the memories of the great spiritual visitations of the years when the work of Mother Ann was a dominant force.

In September 1910, twelve aged Shakers deeded the 1,800 acres of remaining Shaker lands to George Bohon, a resident of Harrodsburg, with the agreement he would care for them until the end of their lives. Sister Mary Settles survived this agreement thirteen years before she too went on to join Mother Ann and her hosts.

Behind them the Shakers left a rich chapter of a vigorous experiment to create the noble society and to bring about by communal effort the perfection of man. The human temple, however, had too many flaws, and the world too many temptations for this to be accomplished. Micajah Burnett and a host of laborers did leave monuments of a high degree of integrity and grace in the village buildings which still survive today and have defied both rough usage and the ravages of time.

Epilogue

SITTING ATOP a plateau overlooking the palisades of the Kentucky River valley, the Shaker Village of Pleasant Hill is surrounded today by 2,700 acres of prime farmland. Once the farm properties of the Shakers were slightly more than 4,000 acres which sustained the community of Believers in comfort and plenty. Thirty-three original buildings have survived civil war, modernization and the ravages of time and hard wear. Their existence today in a state of preservation is little short of miraculous when one considers the extensive litigation which took place, and which involved a heavy burden of indebtedness incurred by aged and senile trustees, in the late 1800s.

In the earlier decades of this century a procession of tenants moved in and out of the buildings, each taking its particular toll of the structures. No tangible fact could attest more eloquently to the integrity of the Shakers as builders than the survival of their handiwork in such solid and durable condition.

The surrounding operating farm today gives the village of Pleasant Hill a safe insulative zone just as it did when the Shakers owned it. Commercial establishments have not crowded up to the village to detract from its serene rural farm setting.

Since the official end of the Society at Pleasant Hill in

1910, the village has undergone a conversion to worldly uses. From 1910 to 1961, Pleasant Hill and its farmland changed owners several times. Tenants who occupied many of the buildings were an assortment, ranging from tobacco sharecroppers, tearoom operators, a Baptist congregation, a country store, and a filling station.

During the Shaker era, use of horse-drawn vehicles made immediate access to a highway a necessity, but with the coming of the automobile, U.S. Highway 68, which ran along the main axis of the village, became a nuisance if not a downright menace to human safety. No longer was Pleasant Hill a calm haven where plain people could live in peace and in harmony with their surroundings, as the Shakers had originally planned. With changing times in the twentieth century there also appeared the stain of neglect and the blighting spirit of shabby worldliness on this once peaceful village.

Prior to the last and successful effort to restore Pleasant Hill to its former condition and the preservation of the village as a monument to both a religious and social past, at least three other efforts were made to renovate it. James Isenberg, an energetic and civic-minded citizen of Harrodsburg, Kentucky, attempted to secure community support for a restoration, but he was unable to generate either funds or energetic public cooperation. Later, the Goodwill Industries undertook to reactivate that part of the village which had been devoted to the various Shaker crafts, but this effort failed also for lack of financial and public interest. Efforts were also made to get the University of Kentucky interested in the acquisition of the land and village and to operate some of its agricultural and vocational programs away from the Lexington farms and campus. Finally, Joseph Graves, a public-spirited Lexington merchant, undertook to create interest in the restoration of the village of Pleasant Hill, but his untimely death postponed for several years the final and successful restoration.

The task of restoring so large a village was herculean and involved shrewd management, planning, skills and crafts, and close supervision. Fortunately, James Lowry Cogar, a native of nearby Woodford County, and the first curator of Colonial Williamsburg, was retained to supervise the restoration. This talented individual was uncompromising in directing the work, and he saw to it that the original Shaker concepts of design, furnishings and taste were faithfully renewed. Local crafts people were employed to renovate and restore the buildings, and to recreate the authentic Shaker interiors and furnishings.

One of the most successful parts of the restoration is the Meeting House. This central structure was used by a Baptist congregation until the plan to restore the village was begun. In order to gain possession of this building it became necessary to deed land outside the village to build the Baptists a new church.

A cardinal tenet of Shaker communal living was industry and ingenuity. In order to accommodate such a large assembly of people and to operate one of the largest and most efficiently run farms in Kentucky during the nineteenth century, the Shakers had to maintain barns, mills, warehouses, shops, and domestic industries. In the restoration of Pleasant Hill several of the shops and their original equipment were refurbished and placed in operation. Also, such structures as the Water House, Post Office, and the Farm Deacon's Shop were restored. Present-day local artisans demonstrate the crafts of weaving and spinning, cooperage, broom making and woodworking.

In 1961, a preservationist viewing Pleasant Hill might have entertained doubts that it could ever be restored to become an important functional landmark of the history of American communal living. Fortunately, a group of public-minded individuals under the leadership of a resourceful and determined Kentucky citizen, Earl D. Wallace, began a crusade to make it not only a monument to a past age of social life, but to convert the village into a viable rural community. In the confused and rapidly changing urban America such an island of unhurried and simple life became even more seductive. By 1963, Wallace and his colleagues had raised sufficient funds to meet general operating expenses, and to purchase options to later buy the village and farm. Within a year the Federal Economic Development Administration granted a loan of $2 million to be repaid over a period of forty years. Today, The Friends of Pleasant Hill come from every state, and some of them have been exceedingly generous in their support.

What was true of the Shakers in the nineteenth century is true of restored Pleasant Hill in the late twentieth century. A large staff is necessary to operate the village. Many weeks throughout the year as many as three to five thousand visitors visit Shaker Village, and approximately the same number patronize the dining room. There are eighty guest rooms in the fifteen of the thirty-three buildings. Instead of recourse to faithful Believers as volunteer laborers, modern Pleasant Hill depends upon a small army of paid employees recruited largely from the two surrounding Kentucky counties of Mercer and Boyle. In background and tradition these people are not wholly different in personalities and local experience from those converts who forsook the world to live under the benign shelter of a communal society.

By force of circumstance, the Shaker Village of Pleasant

The sternwheeler Dixie Belle, of the Port of Shaker Landing, shown as it approaches historic High Bridge train trestle.

Hill carries on the functions of an American village holding conferences, assemblies, exhibits, art and seasonal festivals, and other special events. In 1981 the Corporation purchased a riverboat capable of carrying 150 passengers, and in 1982 it was placed in regular excursion service. This sternwheeler makes its way up the Kentucky River between the picturesque limestone palisades. Not only can visitors make a simulated journey into America's transportation past, they do so amidst a marvel of nature. Geologically the palisades were millions of years in forming, and the river itself flows off a major portion of Appalachian Kentucky.

The dining room at Pleasant Hill with its regional Kentucky dishes is symbolical of the bounty of the rich surrounding farmlands which yielded for the original inhabitants an abundance of grains, fruits, meats, and vegetables. Whatever the Shakers may have been spiritually, they were not self-denying in their dining habits. They and their guests lived well, so well in fact that they were imposed upon by "Winter Shakers" who enjoyed their hospitality without contributing their labors.

Modern visitors to the Shaker Village of Pleasant Hill must remember that in restoring the village members of the board of trustees and advisors attempted to follow as faithfully as possible both the physical and spiritual conformation of the community. Here, once a gathering of dedicated plain people went about their daily tasks and religious worship without fanfare or commotion. Just as important as the authentic restoration of the physical artifacts of the Shakers is the preservation of the serenity of their village and their way of life.

Index

Albany, NY, 6
Alexander, Capt. J. C., 78
Alexander, R. Atchison, 31
Alien and Sedition Laws, 1
American Revolution, 6
Arminius, 3; Arminianism, 4,
Appalachians, 2, 3; Highlands, 1
Asbury, Francis, 2

Baldwin, Tyler, 16, 45
Ballance, Amos, 48, 81
Ballance, James, 74, 78, 79
Ballance, Joanna, 11
Ballance, Willis, 11
Banta, Samuel, 47
Baptists, 2, 6, 63
Barkley, A. M., 92
Barnett, Robert, 28
Bates, Isaacher, 3
Bear Wallow, KY, 76
Beggs, George, 69
Bell, John, 74
Berry, Sam, 81
Bishop Hill, IL, 70, 71
Bloomberg, Andrew, 69, 71
Bluejacket, Chief, 52
Bohon, George, 92
Bowling Green, KY, 76, 78
Bragg, Gen. Braxton, 78
Breckinridge, Capt. W. C. P., 78
Bricky farm, 24

Bridges, Circuit Judge, 47
British colonies, 5
Brooklyn Bridge, 61
Bryant, Benjamin, 48
Bryant, James, 14
Bryant, Jr., John Rufus, 31, 32,
78, 85, 92
Bryant, Paulina, 48
Buckner, Gen. Simon B., 76
Buell, Gen. Don Carlos, 78
Bullard, Harriett, 67
Bunyan, John, Pilgrim's
Progress, 3
Burgin, KY, 69
Burnett, Micajah, 15-20, 48,
63, 92

Calvin, John, 3
Camp Dick Robinson, 76
Cane Ridge, Bourbon
County, 2, 3, Church, 9,
Revival, 2, 3
Castleman, Gen. John B., 92
Cattle importations, 31
Cedar Run, 61
Centre Family, 11, 24, 86, 87
Centre Family House, 16, 69
Centre Family Ministry, 10
Chaplin Hills, 80
Cholera, 63
Cincinnati, OH, 83, 88

Cincinnati, New Orleans and
    Texas Pacific Railroad, 88
Civil War, 29, 34, 37, 69,
    72, 74-82
Clay, Henry, 31, 73
Clay's Ferry Bridge, 77
Cole, Anna, 11
Columbus, KY, 76
Confederacy, 75
Confederate Army, 75, 77-81
Congleton, Virginia, 25
Congress, U.S., 2
Constitutional Convention of
    Kentucky, 1849, 74
Continental Congress, 6
Cornstalk, Chief, 52
Craig, Elijah, 2, Lewis, 2
Crittenden Compromise, 75
Crittenden, John J., 73, 74
Crutcher, Jonas, 68
Cumberland Gap, 2, 3

Daily, Henry, 67, 69, 72, 81, 87
Danville, KY, 78
Day Star, 54
Disciples of Christ, 63
Dix River, 61, 76, 88
Dow, Lorenzo, 23
Dunlavy, Benjamin B., 57, 71, 79,
    80, 85, 86, 90, 91
Dunlavy, John, 3, 4, 9, 22, 23, 25,
    44, 57

East Family, 11, 24, 79, 89
East Family House, 16, 92
Economites, 90
Economy, PA, 70
England, 4, 6
English Durham cattle, 31
Everett, Edward, 74

Falls of the Ohio, 28
Fayette County, KY, 47, 91
Fite, Abram, 28
Flax, 28
Forests in Kentucky, 10
Fourierism, 82
Frankfort, KY, 75, 76, 79
Franklin, Benjamin, 52

Galesburg, IL, 70
Gano, Col. Richard, 80
Gaspar River, KY, 2
*Gass and Banta vs. Wilhite, et. al.
    A Society of Shakers*, 47
Gass, James, 12, 45, 46
"Great Awakening", 2
Gristmill, 28
Guerrillas, 81

Hanes, Richard, 79
Hardman, T. K., 91
Harmony, PA, 70
Harrod, James, 9, 30
Harrodsburg, KY, 10, 74, 76,
    78-81, 87, 92
Harrodsburg Pike, 80
Harrod's Fort, KY, 36
Harrod's Town, KY, 8
Hayes, President Rutherford
    B., 88
Heden, Nils, 71
Hemp, 29, 37, 86
Henry County, IL, 70
Hickman Bridge (Camp
    Nelson), 61
High Bridge, 74, 88
Holy Sinai's Plain, 51, 52
Hooser, Samuel, 58

Indian Creek, 28
Indians, 1, 10, 52-53

Jacobs, Enoch, 54
Janson, Ann Sophia, 71
Janson, Eric, 70, 71
Jansonites, 70, 71
Jefferson County, KY, 91
Jessamine County, KY, 91
Jenkins, Sarah, 48, 85
Johnston, Gen. Albert Sidney, 76
Jones, Sam, 88

Kentucky, 1, 3, 10
    Appellate Court, 48
    beginnings, 9
    cattle sales, 31
    Constitution, 1, 74
    Court of Appeals, 13, 14, 47

Kentucky (continued)
  fairs, 31, 34
  farming, 27
  General Assembly, 12, 44,
    46, 47
  Home Guards, 76
  State Guards, 75, 76
  neutrality, 75
  newspapers, 74
  Revival, 2
Kentucky River, 9, 10, 27, 35, 61,
  74, 76, 88, 92
Kentucky River Gorge, 15, 24
Kincade farm, 25
Kingston, battle of, 77
Kirby-Smith, Gen. Edmund,
  77-79
Ku Klux Klan, 83

La Fayette, Gen. Marquis de, 52
Lebanon, KY, 76, 78
Lee, Mother Ann
  birthday, 60
  death, 7, 49
  earlier life, 4, 5
  founder, 4
  frustrations, 66
  gospel, 9, 22, 46
  in fading times, 90
  imprisonment, 5, 6
  love, 50
  messages, 50
  old ways, 67
  philosophy, 5, 43
  praising of, 58
  teachings, 14, 65, 67
  toils of, 6, 7
  work, 49, 54, 92
Lexington, KY, 10, 68, 74,
  77-80, 92
Lincoln County Circuit Court, 47
Lincoln, President Abraham, 75
Lincoln guns, 76
Liverpool, England, 5
Logan County, KY, 2
Lost Tribes of Israel, 52
Louisville, KY, 73, 75, 78, 83, 87
Louisville Title Company, 92
Lower South, 27, 83

Manchester, England, 4, 5
Manifesto, The, publication, 22
Manson, Gen., 77
Mariah, 5
Marshall, Gen. Humphrey, 79
Marshall, Robert, 3
Mays, Madison M., 90
McAfee brothers, 30
McCarver, Betsey, 25
McGready, James, 2
McGee, John, 2, William, 2
McNemar, Richard, 3, 4, 9, 47, 48
Meacham, John, 11
Meacham, Joseph, 7, 24
Meeting House, 17, 18, 47, 51, 56
Mercer County, KY, 9, 10, 14, 91
Methodists, 2, 63
Mexican War, 73
Miami Valley of Ohio, 3
Millennial Laws, 50
Millennium, 54
Miller, William, 53
Millerites, 54
Mill Springs, battle of, 76
Milton, John, 3, 80
Mississippi River, 27, 29, 76
Morgan, Gen. John Hunt, 76, 77,
  raid, 81
Mulberry trees, 29

Negroes, 68-69, 83
Nelson, Gen. William, 77
Nevada gold mine stock, 90
New England, 7, 8
New Harmony, IN, 44, 70
New Hope, KY, 76
New Lebanon, NY, 3, 4, 6, 14,
  20, 22, 24, 32, 45, 46, 48, 89
New Lebanon Ministry, 18,
  46, 48, 89
"New Light", 4, 9, 22
New Orleans, 27, 63
New Testament, 65
New York, 3, 5, 6
Nicholasville, KY, 61
Niskeyuna, NY, 6
North Carolina, 86
North Family, 11
North Lot Family House, 25, 26

Old Testament, 3, 49
Ohio, 22, 31
Ohio borderland, 74
Ohio River, 1, 2, 27, 28
Ohio Valley, 2, 26
Owen, Robert, 44

Pennebaker, Francis, 63, 85, 90, 91
Pennebaker, William, 63, 85, 89, 91
Penn, William, 52
Perryville, KY, Battle of, 78, 80, 81
Pleasant Hill, (see Shakers)
  administration, 11, 22, 45
  arson, 86
  awareness of outside, 29, 53
  beginning, 9
  boats, 28, 81
  buildings, 15-22, 35
  challenges, 14
  Children's Order, 63
  Christmas, 7, 52, 60
  Civil War, 75-82
  Civil War stragglers, 78
  classes, 23, 24
  common ownership, 46-47
  community, 9-12, 14, 22, 27, 43-45
  converts, 5, 7-9, 21, 23, 25, 26, 31, 59, 86
  covenant, 9, 11, 14, 23, 48
  dances, 57, 58
  debts, 86, 92
  dishonesty in, 89
  divorce, 13
  domain, 10
  economics, 41
  farming, 27-34, implements, 33
  Gathering Order, 24-26, 63
  gifts, imaginary, 50, 53
  horses, 33, 81
  labor, 42
  land, 10
  litigation, 46-47
  livestock, 30, 34, 83
  mills, 16, 28, 34, 83
  ministry, 10, 11, 22

organization, 11, 12, 23, 43
pacifists, 12, 13
panic of 1819, 44
prosperity, 73, 74
public meetings, 58, 59
recruits, 22, 66, 67, 71, 72, 85
reforms, 45-46
secluded holy place, 51, 52
sheep, 32
Sisters, 39-41
spiritualism, 49-54
successes, 21, 34, 48, 74, 82
temptations, 60
tenor of life, 55, 56, 83
Thanksgiving Day, 52, 60
village, 15, 26, 27
"Winter Shakers", 69
woodworking, 34-38
Polk, Gen. 76
Poole, Sarah, 49, 50
Powhatan, Chief, 52
Presbyterians, 2-4, 63
Proselyting, 22, 62-64, 66, 85

Quakers, 5, 73

Rankin, James, 48, 85
Rankin, John, 2
Rapp, George, 44, 70
Rees, E. J., 83
Revival, 2, 6
Revolutionary War, 1, 6
Runyon, George, 71
Rupe, Sarah, 91

St. Louis, MO, 83
Salt River, 9
Sanders, Lewis, 31
Scotland, 31
Scott, Elhanon W., 48, 81, 85
Settles, Mary, 92
Shakers, (see Pleasant Hill)
  agricultural changes, 86
  agriculture, 30
  anti-war, 75
  apostates, 46-48, 66, 67
  Believers, 6, 8, 12, 14, 21, 32, 58
  breakdown of discipline, 67

102

Shakers *(continued)*
  brooms, 29, 38, 63
  bulls, "Shaker" 31,
    "Orizimbo" 31
  catering to travelers, 68, 69, 88
  celibacy, 5, 6, 9, 12, 18, 56, 60,
    67, 71
  cemetery, 50
  changing America, 81-83
  children, 12-13, 26, 62-65
  Chinese sugar cane, 34
  Church order, 23
  classes, 23, 24
  cloth trade, 28
  clothing, 39, 40
  cobblers, 37
  colonizing, 8
  communities, 3, 7, 8, 62
  cooking, 40-41
  cordwainers, 37
  craft shops, 35-37
  craftsmen, 26, 35
  crime, 67
  distilled spirits, 50
  doctrine, 7
  education, 64-65, 87
  ethics, 73
  fabrics, 28, 29
  family divisions, 11, 24, 90
  farms, 28-29
  ferry, 28, 88
  foods, 40, 41
  furniture, 35-37
  gardeners, 30
  garden seed, 29, 30, 63
  garments, 40
  golden age, 73
  herbs, 40, 64
  hogs, 32, "Black Hawk", 32
  horses, mules, 33
  hospitality, 67-69
  inventions, 28, 33, 38, 39
  journals, 26, 37, 60, 66-68,
    74, 79
  Landing on the river, 28, 60,
    61, 88
  lands, 34, 90-91
  mechanical competition, 42
  medicinal materials, 40

  missionaries, 3, 9
  national politics, 74-75
  Negroes, 68, 83
  neighbors, 28
  novitiates, 23-25
  peddlars, 29
  post-war, 72, 82-84, decline,
    67, 87-92
  public attitudes, 26
  preserves and syrups, 34, 41
  railroad influence, 87
  readmissions, 67
  recreation, 60-61
  runaways, 65
  Sabbatarians, 23, 56
  sale of products, 42
  secession, 75
  separation of sexes, 56-57, 63
  singing, 57-59
  Sisters, 39, 40, 55, 57, 62, 64,
    80, 81
  slavery, 68, 74
  spinning, weaving, 39, 42
  social philosophy, 43
  textiles, 28, 40
  theological beliefs, 43
  theology, 22, 23
  tobacco, pork, tea, coffee ban,
    40, 50
  Unionists, 74
  villages, 8
  wares, 37-39
  waterworks, 38
  worship, 17-19, 23-24, 56, 58,
    59, 88

Shain, Dr. John, 40, 63
"Shaking Quakers," 5
Shawnee Run, 9, 10, 28, 81
Shawnee Run Family
  Covenant, 11
Sherman, Gen. William T., 88
Shields, Joel, 31
Shiloh, battle of, 77
Silkworms, 29, 30
Smith, Lucy, 11, 44
Smith, Joseph, 52
Society of Believers, 7, 8, 14, 29,
  33, 34, 43, 66, 82

Society of Shakers, 8, 15
South Carolina, 29, 75
South Union, KY, 62, 85, 90
Spiral staircase in Trustees'
  Office, 19, 20
"Spirit of New Lebanon," 4
Springfield, KY, 76
Standerin, Abraham, 5
Stone, Barton W., 3, 9, 23
Sutton, Jane, 92
Swedes, 70-72, 86
Sweden, 72, 86

Taylor, John, 2
Tecumseh, Chief, 52
3rd Pennsylvania Cavalry, 76
Thomas, Elisha, homestead, 9,
  10, 24
Thompson, John, 3
Tobacco, 50, 86, 88
Tompkinsville, KY, 76
Trustees' Office, 19, 51, 80, 88
Turner, Samuel, 11, 44, 48

Union Village, OH, 22, 31, 32,
  47, 90
Utopia, 82

Valley of Virginia, 3, 8
Varner, Louis, farm, 24
Versailles Pike, 80
Voris, Francis, 14, 28

Wabash River, IN, 44
War Department, 76
War of 1812, 12
Washington, Gen. George, 52
Watervliet, NY, 7, 49
Watson, Oliver, 90, litigation, 91
Wayne, Gen. Anthony, 1
Western American frontier, 1, 8
West Family, 11, 24, 26, 77, 89
West Family House, 16, 24, 26
West Lot Family, 25, 90
West Lot Family House, 26
West Union, IN, 44
Whitbey, John, 44
Whitewater, OH, 69
Whittaker, James, 7
Whittymore, Carolyn, 65
Whittymore, James, 65
Wickliffe, Robert, 47
Wildcat, battle of, 76
Wilhite, Abram, 12, 14
Woodburn farm, 31
Worley, Malcolm, 3, 4, 9
Wright, Lucy, 7

Young, Elizabeth, 54
Youngs, Benjamin, 9

Zion, 80
Zoarites, 90

ABOUT THE AUTHORS

A Kentuckian by adoption, an outstanding teacher, a prolific writer, Thomas D. Clark was born in Mississippi in 1903. A graduate of the University of Mississippi, he came to the University of Kentucky for his master's degree in history. After being awarded a Ph.D. in history by Duke University, he became a faculty member at UK in 1931. In 1942, he was appointed head of the history department, remaining there until 1965, at which time he was named Distinguished Professor of History Emeritus. After retiring from UK, he taught at Indiana University and Eastern Kentucky University.

He has served as a Fulbright lecturer at Oxford University, NATO professor at the University of Athens and the University of Thessalonika, Greece; and has lectured also in India and Yugoslavia.

In addition to teaching Dr. Clark was active in collecting and organizing, for the University of Kentucky, a modern Kentucky Archives, and in establishing the University Press of Kentucky.

His long-standing interest in Kentucky history, his knowledge of the Shakers, his devotion to the restoration of Pleasant Hill, all combined with his skill as a writer make this volume both a readable scholarly work and a labor of love.

The text of this book is based largely upon the research F. Gerald Ham did on the Shakers for his master's degree at the University of Kentucky. Dr. Ham is now State Archivist of Wisconsin.